PRO TACTICS™ SERIES

PRO TACTICS™

CATFISH

*Use the Secrets of the Pros to
Catch More and Bigger Catfish*

Keith "Catfish" Sutton

THE LYONS PRESS
Guilford, Connecticut
An imprint of The Globe Pequot Press

To MARK DAVIS, A TRUE FRIEND,
ALWAYS THERE, ALWAYS EXTENDING A HELPING HAND.

The Lyons Press is an imprint of The Globe Pequot Press.
Pro Tactics is a trademark of Morris Book Publishing, LLC.

Photos by Keith Sutton unless otherwise noted.

Illustrations by Michael Gellatly

Text design by Peter Holm, Sterling Hill Productions

Library of Congress Cataloging-in-Publication Data is available.

ISBN 978-1-59921-301-9

Printed in the United States of America

10 9 8 7 6 5 4 3 2 1

CONTENTS

My love of catfishing began at the impressionable age of ten when my Uncle Pat invited all his nieces and nephews to fish a pond he had stocked with thousands of channel catfish. The pond had been off limits since its creation while Uncle Pat fattened the cats on a prodigious diet of commercial fish chow. His intent was to create a kids-only fishing paradise teeming with big, hungry, easy-to-catch catfish, and that he did. I will never forget standing on the pond's bank with my sister and cousins on opening day and catching one big catfish after another. As soon as we would drop in a baited hook, a whiskerfish would gobble it up, and our long cane pole would bend under the fish's weight. Until that day, none of us had caught a fish bigger than a bluegill, so we were excited as we struggled to beach cats as big as 10 pounds. All of us went home very happy, including Uncle Pat, whose joy that day knew no bounds.

For most of my cousins, that day was a one-shot deal. Few of them ever visited the pond again. For me, it was just the beginning. I fished the pond almost daily, and the more catfish I caught, the more I wanted to catch.

Not surprisingly, big cats soon drew most of my attention. Uncle Pat had stocked several brood fish in the pond, and one of these—a 20-pounder—broke my line on several occasions. I fished for her after school, and she taught me a lot about the habits of catfish.

She usually hung out by a big stump, and I learned she was keenly attuned to the world around her. If I walked the shore toward the stump at a normal gait, she would shoot away before I got close enough to cast a bait. If I approached quietly, I still had to be sure not to cast a shadow on the water, or once again she would spook. She taught me that big cats are wary cats. Only the stealthiest approach would allow me to dangle a bait within her reach. When finally I caught her, I quickly released her so I might enjoy the experience once again. And the tenth time I landed her was as exciting as the first.

Every time I learned something about catfish behavior, my fascination grew. I started fishing other lakes and rivers and began reading everything I could find about catfish. The thought never entered my young mind that one day I'd be writing a book on the subject.

You have in your hands my third such book, more than four decades of experience bound together between two covers. I hope you learn many new things as you delve into its pages. Most of all, I hope all your catfishing adventures are fruitful and create memories that will last a lifetime.

CHAPTER ONE

The Truth about Catfish

Right up front, we should try to dispel some myths about catfish you may have heard. Some of these ugly rumors are as persistent as the old wives' tale about toads causing warts. The truth may be much different.

What you may have heard: Catfish are strictly bottom-feeders.
The truth: Catfish are well adapted for feeding on the bottoms of rivers, lakes, and ponds, but if you think they never feed at mid-depths or on the surface, you're wrong. Catfish are opportunistic and take their food where they find it. They often feed on grasshoppers, cicadas, frogs, and other creatures found on the surface (floating catfish chow too), and prey on baitfish such as shad and herring in midwaters. If bottom-fishing doesn't produce, try presenting elsewhere in the water column.

What you may have heard: Catfish are lazy scavengers that only eat dead, rotten foods.
The truth: Catfish, particularly young catfish, will eat some dead and decaying food items, but they also are highly efficient predators adept at chasing down and ambushing live prey.

There are many persistent myths about catfish, including one whopper about monster cats near dams that are large enough to swallow divers.

What you may have heard: Divers working on dams have seen incredibly large catfish—so large, in fact, that the divers refused to go back under water because they feared being eaten.

The truth: This tale surfaces frequently throughout the country, but it's just not true. While some catfish can weigh more than 100 pounds, they don't get big enough to swallow humans. One indication these stories are nothing but myths is the fact that the people telling them aren't the ones who saw the catfish. It's always some anonymous person or a friend of a friend who isn't available for verification. That's a key element of all such myths.

What you may have heard: The smellier the bait, the better it is for catfish.

The truth: Catfish anglers have been mixing up smelly brews of secret-recipe specialty baits for centuries, and these "stinkbaits" can be great cat-catchers. Stinkbaits don't work because they stink, however. In fact, what stinks to anglers can't be smelled by catfish; the chemistry of olfaction is much different in catfish and humans. The truth is, many superb catfish baits stink no more than baits used for walleyes or bass.

A catfish's whiskers, or barbels, are harmless. They're organs of taste, not organs of defense.

What you may have heard: A catfish's whiskers and spines are poisonous stingers.

The truth: The whiskers, or barbels, of catfish often are avoided because people believe they can sting. Actually, the barbels are as limp as cooked spaghetti and can't hurt you. These fleshy organs are covered with dense taste buds to help cats find food. Catfish *can* inflict painful wounds with their sharp, serrated pectoral and dorsal fin spines. On madtoms and saltwater catfish, the spines' skin contains poison cells that rupture when an unwary angler gets stabbed. The wounds are very painful and often require medical attention. The spines of channel, blue, and flathead catfish are not covered with poison cells, but painful puncture wounds can occur when handling these fish. The wounds may become infected if not properly treated.

What you may have heard: If a catfish sees your hook, it won't bite.

The truth: Catfish don't look at a hook and think, "I better not bite that or I might get caught." In fact, you'll probably catch more cats if you leave the barb of the hook exposed.

What you may have heard: Catfish thrive in muddy, often foul water.

The truth: Catfish can tolerate poor-quality water that might kill other species, and are able to feed in warm, muddy water that would stress many creatures. But just like smallmouth bass, trout and other fishes, catfish need clean water in which to thrive. If the water is too turbid, too hot, too polluted, or too low in oxygen, catfish will not be in prime condition.

What you may have heard: The best fishing for catfish is during summer.

The truth: Catfishing can be great during hot weather, particularly at night or near dawn and dusk. Summer, however, is not the best season for catfishing. Anglers who learn to find and pattern catfish during other seasons often discover the bite is even better when the water, and the weather, is cooler. Catfishing during winter often produces more and bigger fish than fishing in warm months.

What you may have heard: Catfish only bite at night.

The truth: Catfish feed around the clock—morning, noon, and night. In clear water, the bite may be better during hours of darkness. The more turbid the water, the more likely the bite will be good when the sun is high.

What you may have heard: Catfish are dumb compared to other fishes.

The truth: A study conducted by Missouri fisheries biologist Gordon Farabee tested the comparative learning ability of different fishes. Catfish learned quickest and achieved the highest overall scores, far above other popular sportfish such as bass, trout, pike, and bluegills.

What you may have heard: Catfish make their croaking sounds using their swim bladder.

The truth: The swim bladder does not produce the unusual vocalizations of North American catfish. The sounds are made when the catfish moves the fins on the sides of its body. The bony spine in each pectoral fin has an enlarged base that rubs adjacent bones to produce the catfish's weird voice. Many species vocalize in this manner.

CHAPTER TWO

The Catfishes

Catfish comprise an incredibly large and diverse group of animals—much larger, in fact, than most people realize. To date, 2,855 species have been described. This means that one in four species of all freshwater fishes is a catfish. One in ten species of all fishes—marine and freshwater—is a catfish. And one in twenty species of all vertebrates is a catfish.

Even with this large number of documented species, scientists estimate another 873 to 1,750 species of catfish remain to be described. These new species are represented by specimens of recognized, but still unnamed, fishes in institutional collections or are predicted to be discovered through additional field research under way in many parts of the world. Within the next few years, the number of recognized catfish species is predicted to climb to between 3,600 and 4,500.

North America north of Mexico is home to just forty-five catfish species, quite a meager collection compared to other continents. But what we lack in quantity, we make up for in quality. The "big three" of North American catfish—channel, blue, and flathead—rank among the world's largest. Other species popular with American anglers include the white catfish and several species of bullhead.

When you're fishing, it's important to understand that each species of catfish exhibits unique behaviors. Blue cats are different from channel cats, channel cats are different from flatheads, and so forth. Understanding the differences helps us target each species properly, thus increasing our success rate and allowing us to better enjoy each precious hour on the water. The descriptions below will help you get started.

Channel Catfish (*Ictalurus punctatus*)

Let's begin our discussion of North American catfish with the most popular, most widespread, most abundant member of the family, the channel cat. Blue cats and flatheads grow much larger, but when it comes to popularity polls, these heavyweights can't hold a candle to their cousin. The channel catfish is the most popular fish in three states (Iowa, Kansas, and Nebraska), second most popular in two (Arkansas and Mississippi), and third most popular in ten (Alabama, Arizona, Colorado, Illinois, Kentucky, Missouri,

Channel catfish are one of the most widespread and popular sportfish in North America.

Nevada, Ohio, Oklahoma, and Texas). Everywhere it swims, the channel cat is targeted by a devoted group of anglers who like nothing better than catching this whiskered wonder.

There are good reasons why millions of folks love channel cats, chief among them the fact that this fish always seems hungry and eager to bite. Everyone can catch them—young anglers and old, skilled and unskilled. And fun catching it is. These sleek, muscular fish do their best to throw a hook, and that bulldoggish ferocity puts smiles on the faces of all anglers. Regardless of when you fish for them—day or night; spring, summer, fall, or winter—chances are you'll catch a mess.

Channel cats are delicious, too. No matter how the cook prepares them—deep-fried, broiled, baked, grilled, or in a chowder—they provide the makings for some of the most mouthwatering repasts imaginable. And your fellow catfishing enthusiasts won't look down their noses at you while you're cleaning a stringer full of small fish for the table. For most catfish anglers, eating the catch is part of the joy of fishing.

Other Local Names

Spotted cat, speckled cat, blue cat, blue channel, fiddler, lady cat, chucklehead, willow cat

Description

Channel cats are sleeker and more pleasing to the eye than flatheads and blues. Most have silvery-gray to coppery-brown back and sides, and a white belly. The tail is deeply forked. The sides usually are peppered with a few to many small black spots. Breeding males are deep blue-black, with thickened, fleshy lips and a knobby, swollen head.

The look-alike blue catfish has similar coloration and a deeply forked tail, but always lacks the scattered dark spots seen on most channel cats. The spots may be absent on older channel cats, however, so they do not provide a reliable means for separating the two species. The most precise method for distinguishing channels and blues is looking at the anal fin. If it has a straight outer edge and thirty or more rays,

Channel catfish. DUANE RAVER, USFWS

it's a blue cat. If the fin has twenty-four to twenty-nine rays and is rounded, it's a channel catfish. White catfish, another look-alike, usually have fewer than twenty-four rays in the anal fin and a less deeply forked tail.

Size

Channel cats are midsize models as catfish go. An average weight in most waters with healthy populations is 1 to 5 pounds, but 6- to 10-pounders are common throughout the fish's range. Channel cats weighing 15 pounds or more are caught only occasionally except in a few extraordinary waters. In the Red River below Lockport Dam near Selkirk, Manitoba, for example, 20- to 25-pound channel cats comprise a large percentage of the catch.

The 47½-inch-long world record caught in South Carolina's Lake Moultrie in July 1964 weighed 58 pounds, but this was an exceptional

Channel cats larger than 30 pounds are rare in all but a few waters.

fish, and most experts agree this record is unlikely ever to be broken. Channel cats heavier than 50 pounds have been reported only in four states—South Carolina, Arkansas, Mississippi, and California—and no body of water has regularly produced channels that size. In all but a few waters, a 20-pounder is considered a trophy, and 30-pounders are as rare as 12-pound largemouths.

Range

Channel cats are the most widely distributed sportfish in North America. They originally were native to waters between the Rocky and Appalachian Mountains from the Hudson Bay drainage to the Gulf of Mexico and waters north and east of the Appalachians. Introductions expanded their range to include every state but Alaska, plus six of the ten Canadian provinces and many lakes and rivers in Mexico as well. Today, channel cats are considered important sport species in at least thirty-two U.S. states.

Habitat

These fish inhabit everything from city ponds, gravel-bottomed creeks, and muddy bayous to vast man-made reservoirs, natural lakes, and big delta rivers. They can tolerate extreme conditions better than many fish, but they do not, as many people think, prefer living in turbid, poor-quality waters. Channel catfish are healthiest in clean, warm, well-oxygenated water with slow to moderate current and abundant cover such as logs, boulders, cavities, and debris. Their adaptability is amazing, however, and channel cats inhabit nearly every body of water within their range that's not too cold or too polluted.

Diet

Channel catfish sometimes eat plant foods such as algae, seeds, and fruits, but their diet consists primarily of aquatic and semiaquatic animals. The diet changes as the catfish grow. Fry eat zooplankton and small aquatic insects. Juvenile fish to about 12 inches long feed extensively on large aquatic insects but also eat terrestrial insects, crayfish, mussels, and small fish. Channel cats longer than 12 inches incorporate more fish in their diet, but still depend heavily on invertebrates and other available foods. The bigger they become, though, the more fish they eat. By the time a channel cat weighs several pounds, it subsists almost entirely on other fish.

Channel catfish are generalists and use food items in proportion to their availability. This means the diet may change from season to season as different foods become obtainable. For example, in summer, channel cats may feed heavily on grasshoppers, cicadas, and other large insects that are abundant in this season. If rising water floods woodlands where terrestrial crayfish live, channel cats move into the flooded forests to take advantage of this bounty. When large numbers of frogs enter the water to breed and lay eggs, they are eagerly consumed by hungry catfish. And so forth.

Know, too, that channel catfish feed very little, sometimes not at all, when engaged in spawning activities—an important fact to file away for future reference. And while channels can be caught even during the coldest days and nights of winter, they feed much less often when the water temperature drops below 48 degrees F.

This blue cat weighs 72 pounds. The species has the potential to grow more than twice this size.

Blue Catfish (*Ictalurus furcatus*)

No catfish in North America grows larger than the blue. The only freshwater fishes in the U.S. that reach larger maximum sizes are the alligator gar, lake sturgeon, and white sturgeon, but none of these is nearly as widespread and abundant as the blue catfish. Anglers hoping to catch a freshwater fish weighing 50 to 100 pounds or more are turning their attention to this incredible catfish in greater numbers than ever before. As a result, dozens of new state and world records have been established in the past two decades.

A proper telling of the blue cat story should start with a historical note recorded by William Heckman in *Steamboating Sixty-Five Years on Missouri's Rivers* (1950). "Of interest to fishermen," Heckman said, "is the fact that the largest known fish ever caught in the Missouri River was taken just below Portland, Missouri. This fish, caught in 1866, was a blue channel cat and weighed 315 lb. It provided the biggest sensation of those days all through Chamois and Morrison Bottoms. Another 'fish sensation' was brought in about 1868 when two men, Sholten and New, brought into Hermann, Missouri, a blue channel cat that tipped the scales at 242 lb."

This note indicates blue cats, often known then and now as "blue channel cats," once reached much larger sizes than today's fish. The world rod-and-reel record currently stands at 124 pounds, but blue cats exceeding 100 pounds are rare in the twenty-first century. By comparison, published accounts from Heckman and others provide evidence that it was common to catch blue catfish weighing 125 to 250 pounds from big Midwestern rivers during the nineteenth century.

Overharvest accounted for the decline of big blue cats in many areas. A sizeable catfish brought a good price at the fish market, and there were no harvest restrictions in most areas. The primary factor, however, was river "improvement" work begun after World War II. Dams blocked natural

Overharvest of mature blue cats for fish markets was one factor that led to the decline of heavyweight blues in many areas by the middle of the nineteenth century.

migration routes, and channelization reduced spawning and feeding areas. As the big river systems they inhabited were altered, blue cat populations plummeted. Anglers seeking big blues were increasingly frustrated by too few fish and a lack of trophy-class specimens.

When Edward Elliott landed a 97-pound world record in the South Dakota portion of the Missouri River in 1957, it seemed his fish was the last of the giants. More than three decades would pass before a heavier blue cat was caught on rod and reel.

Changes first were noticed in the 1970s and 1980s when introductions expanded the blue cat's range from California to the Carolinas. Many lakes were stocked where blues previously were absent. And the huge size of the fish in many of these waters sparked renewed interest in trophy blue cat fishing. Big river fish started turning up, too—most on trotlines—including a 118-pounder from Arkansas' Big Creek, 120-pound blues in Texas and Oklahoma, and a 128-pounder in Louisiana.

Perhaps blues started adapting to habitat changes. Perhaps decreased fishing pressure allowed them to grow. No one knows for sure, but more anglers began seeking these freshwater giants.

One highlight of the blue cat's comeback came on March 14, 1991. While fishing in the Tail Race Canal below South Carolina's Lake Moultrie that day, George Lijewski landed a 109-pound, 4-ounce blue, a new world record. After thirty-two years, Ed Elliott's record had fallen.

Other records fell during the 1990s as well—state records, that is. Three giants were among the catches: a 103-pound Missouri record from the Missouri River, a 104-pound Indiana/Kentucky record from the Ohio River, and a 105-pound Mississippi River blue that established a new benchmark for Louisiana. Anglers in Mississippi and Virginia caught new state-record blues at least three times during the decade; California, Indiana, Iowa, North Carolina, Oklahoma, Tennessee, and Texas records fell twice; and new records also were established in Alabama, Florida, Illinois, and New Mexico.

This surge in record activity and Lijewski's catch had folks thinking: "Could the world record fall again?"

Indeed. On July 5, 1996, William McKinley landed a 111-pound world-record blue in Alabama's Wheeler Reservoir. And to no one's surprise, two years later, on June 7, 1998, a 112-pounder from Tennessee's Cumberland River established yet another benchmark.

The year 2000 had hardly begun when the first "century-mark" blue of the new millennium was reported in California. Roger Rohrbouck caught that 101-pound behemoth on March 12, 2000, in southern California's 1,000-acre San Vicente Reservoir, proving that waters outside the blue cat's natural range also had record potential.

Once again anglers were speculating on the possibility of a new world record being caught, and once again it happened. On August 3, 2001, Charles Ashley Jr. landed a whopping 116-pound, 12-ounce blue cat on the Mississippi River at West Memphis, Arkansas. Ashley's record was short-lived, however. It stood just over two years until Cody Mullenix of Howe, Texas, caught a monster weighing 121 pounds, 8 ounces in the Texas portion of Lake Texoma. Landed on January 16, 2004, that blue cat, which Mullenix named Splash, was exhibited for two years at the Texas Freshwater Fisheries Center in Athens. The International Game Fish Association (IGFA) certified the fish as a new all-tackle world record in May 2004, but one year later, that record, too, would be broken.

The date was May 21, 2005. Fishing below Melvin Price Lock and Dam on the Mississippi River at Alton, Illinois, Tim Pruitt hooked a blue

Illinois angler Tim Pruitt with his 124-pound, world-record blue catfish. ILLINOIS DEPT. OF NATURAL RESOURCES

cat that was 58 inches long with a 44-inch girth. That catfish, the currently recognized IGFA world record, weighed an even 124 pounds.

Could even bigger blue cats be swimming somewhere? The probability is high. And that fact has made the blue cat the target of thousands of anglers, each of whom hopes to be the next person to put their name in the record books.

Other Local Names

White cat, silver cat, blue fulton, white fulton, blue channel, humpback cat, highfin blue, forktail cat

Description

Although they grow much larger, blue catfish closely resemble channel cats. The back and sides are slate-blue to grayish-brown, fading to a whitish belly. The tail is deeply forked. On blue cats, however, the anal fin contains more rays—usually thirty to thirty-five as compared to the channel cat's twenty-four to twenty-nine—and has a straight and tapered outer margin (not rounded) much like a barber's comb. In muddy environs, some blue cats appear albinistic, the pale skin evoking the common nickname "white cat." Many individuals also are distinctly humpbacked in appearance and have a head much smaller in proportion to the body than a similar-size channel cat.

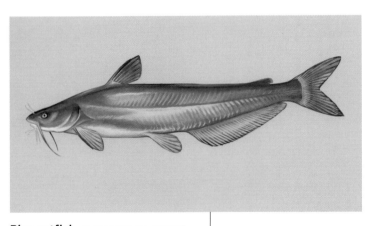

Blue catfish. DUANE RAVER, USFWS

Size

Healthy populations of blue cats usually contain numerous individuals up to 28 inches, or about 10 pounds. Larger, older fish are much less common, but in some prime waters, catching several 20- to 40-pound blues during a few hours of fishing is not considered unusual during peak fishing times. The largest specimens, those weighing 50 pounds or more, are scarce and often difficult to find and catch, but more and more anglers enjoy the challenge of targeting these big, hard-hitting trophies.

Range

Blue catfish occur in portions of at least twenty-nine states, from South

Dakota to southern Texas and from Washington to Florida. They're also found throughout the eastern third of Mexico and south into Guatemala and Belize. The native range encompasses the major rivers of the Mississippi, Ohio, and Missouri basins of the central and southern U.S. Blues have been introduced in Washington, Oregon, California, Arizona, Colorado, Maryland, Virginia, South Carolina, and Florida.

In some areas at the fringe of their range—West Virginia and Minnesota, for instance—blue catfish are so rare they're considered a species of special concern. They are also uncommon over much of the northern part of their range, a decline triggered by commercial fishing, dam construction, and stream channelization.

Habitat

Blue catfish prefer open waters of large reservoirs and main channels, backwaters, and bays of large rivers where water normally is turbid. Given the opportunity, they spend much of their time in deep, swift channels and flowing pools. Large specimens often hold in the swift tailwaters below dams. Although sometimes stocked in ponds and small reservoirs, blue cats thrive better in large, open-water impoundments, especially those with gizzard shad as forage. Blue cats also tolerate moderate levels of salinity and are found in brackish-water marshes and rivers in some coastal areas.

Diet

Blue cats are opportunistic feeders, consuming a variety of animals that include fishes, insects, crayfish, and freshwater mussels. Larger individuals eat mostly fish and larger invertebrates. They are particularly fond of shad, herring, and other schooling baitfish and often are found associated with these schools. Blue cats frequently suspend in deep water beneath gizzard shad being eaten by striped bass, picking off the wounded and dead shad left by the stripers. They also feed on wounded baitfish that pass through the turbines of dams and baitfish killed by cold winter temperatures.

Blues fall somewhere between the other two species of big cats in feeding habits, not insisting on live baits as flatheads do but generally ignoring many specialty offerings such as stinkbaits and blood baits often used to catch channel cats. Blue cats feed year-round except during spawning activities. Feeding diminishes, however, when the water temperature falls below 40 degrees F.

Flathead Catfish (*Pylodictis olivaris*)

The flathead is a brute of a fish, muscular and streamlined, but ugly by all accepted standards. Its flattened cranium looks like it was run through a trash compactor. The beady eyes are wide-set. Its thickened underlip protrudes in a perpetual pout, wormlike barbels dangle from its chin and mouth, and its hide has the color and texture of a slug.

Despite its ugliness, however, the flathead catfish has a devoted following of anglers. This is largely because this fish is a big, bullish battler. When one takes your bait, you may first think you have snagged a sunken log. But set the hook, and it will explode with a fury that is sometimes frightening. The unprepared angler may see his rod snapped like a strand of dry spaghetti or stand in amazement after his favorite fishing combo has been yanked from his hands and deep-sixed.

The biggest flatheads I've seen—50- to 80-pounders—were bizarrely obese, with enormous potbellies. Thin barbels dangled from the corners

Flathead catfish are aptly named. The flat, broadened head is a key characteristic distinguishing this catfish from its relatives.

of cavernous mouths like Fu Manchu mustaches. Beady eyes glared menacingly from barbarous, battle-hardened facades. Like Sumo wrestlers, they gave the distinct impression that anyone foolish enough to mess with them might come away minus an arm or leg.

Giant flatheads are like Sumos in other ways, too. They move with a fluidity and swiftness that seems contradictory to their corpulence. I once watched a 30-pounder in an aquarium devour a saucer-size bluegill in a single gulp. It happened in a split second. The flathead darted from a hollow log, flared its gills, and inhaled the sunfish.

"Never knew what hit him," another observer proclaimed about the unfortunate bluegill. "Good thing flatheads don't get big as killer whales. None of us would be safe in the water."

Indeed, the flathead is one of the most formidable predators in freshwater. And few experiences in the world of angling can compare to catching a trophy-class specimen.

Other Local Names

Shovelhead cat, yellow cat, mud cat, goujon, Appaloosa cat, Opelousas or Op cat, Johnnie cat, bashaw

Description

A broad, flattened head gives the flathead its common name. The color of the back and sides can vary considerably, from pale yellow to dark brown or black, but most specimens are olive-green or yellowish-brown with distinct mottling. The belly is pale yellow to cream-white. The tail is only slightly notched, not deeply forked like the tails of channel and blue catfish. The lower jaw protrudes beyond the upper, also unlike channels and blues. Young fish sometimes are confused with bullheads, but the tooth pad on the flathead's upper jaw has a crescent-shaped backward extension on each side that is absent on bullheads.

Flathead catfish. DUANE RAVER, USFWS

Size

The all-tackle world record is a 123-pound flathead caught in Kansas's Elk City Reservoir in May 1998. This is one of very few flatheads over

100 pounds ever documented, and the only one caught on rod and reel. One larger specimen—a 139-pound, 14-ounce flathead—was caught on a snagline in the Arkansas River near Little Rock, Arkansas, in May 1982, so there is evidence a new world record could be caught in the future. Even so, that possibility seems remote.

Flatheads are extremely fast-growing, with tag returns indicating that even larger, older fish may put on as much as 10 pounds annually in prime waters. A yearly weight gain of 2 to 5 pounds is typical for a flathead between ages three and eight.

Thirty- to 50-pound flatheads are caught often enough in many lakes and rivers that they hardly warrant notice, and while bigger fish are much less common, they are available in many blue-ribbon waters throughout the fish's range. Few freshwater big-game fish offer anglers such outstanding opportunities for catching the fish of a lifetime. And when a mess of fish for the dinner table is the goal, the abundance of small flatheads in many waters makes it a cinch to load a cooler with plenty of "eaters."

Range

Flathead catfish are native to Middle America, primarily the Mississippi, Mobile, and Rio Grande river drainages and the Great Lakes region. They also occur naturally in northeastern portions of Mexico. The species has been widely introduced into waters outside its native range, including lakes and/or rivers in Arizona, California, Colorado, Florida, Georgia, Idaho, Oregon, Pennsylvania, North Carolina, South Carolina, Virginia, Washington, and Wyoming.

Habitat

Although found in both lakes and rivers, flatheads are generally considered river fish. They are most abundant in large, sluggish, deep river pools, usually over hard bottoms or where silt deposition is slow. They generally avoid heavy current, but sometimes feed in swift water at the ends of dikes and in tailraces below dams. Big specimens seldom are found in creeks, ponds, and small lakes, but populations are substantial in many larger reservoirs and natural lakes within their range.

Flatheads love cover. During daylight hours, they usually seek shelter around or within submerged logs, piles of driftwood, toppled trees, snags, and cavities in middepths. At night they leave these sanctuaries and move into more open, shallower waters to feed. Adults tend to be solitary and often are aggressive toward others of their kind. Thus, a single spot of cover usually yields only one, or at most two or three, adult flatheads.

Diet

Young flatheads feed heavily on invertebrates, especially crayfish. As the fish grow, however, they gradually turn to a diet comprised largely of other fish, including shad, sunfish, suckers, and other catfish. Unlike channel cats and blues, flatheads scavenge very little and prefer live foods. Adult flatheads rarely are caught on chicken liver, commercial baits, or cut-baits, which frequently are used for tempting their cousins.

Flatheads feed year-round in more temperate climes, but cease feeding when carrying out spawning activities and feed little or not at all when the water temperature falls below about 45 degrees F.

Brushpiles and other dense woody cover are favorite haunts of big flatheads.

White Catfish (*Ameiurus catus*)

No large North American catfish are more misunderstood than the white cat. Many anglers confuse them with blues and channel cats, a situation compounded by the fact that blue cats in many areas are commonly called "white cats."

White cats are similar to other species in many respects, which also adds to the muddle. They're built like bullheads and colored like blue cats, and larger specimens look almost identical to channel cats without spots. White cats even confuse scientists. At one time, they were considered more closely related to channel cats than bullheads and were placed in the scientific genus *Ictalurus* with channel cats and blues. Later, they were moved to the genus *Ameiurus* with bullheads.

Despite the confusion, white catfish are certainly worthy of the angler's attention. These scrappy fish are common in many waters throughout their range. They're aggressive, fun to catch (especially on light tackle), and eagerly take a wide variety of baits. In parts of southern New England, they are the only catfish commonly caught except bullheads.

Other Local Names

Forktail cat, Potomac cat, Schuylkill catfish

Description

The white cat's back and upper sides are light blue-gray to dark slate-gray, fading to a whitish belly. The tail is somewhat forked, but the lobes

White catfish. DUANE RAVER, USFWS

of the tail aren't as sharply pointed as are those of the channel catfish and may be rounded in older fish. The head is very broad and blunt. The best way to distinguish white cats from look-alike blues and channel cats is to examine the chin barbels and count the anal fin rays. The barbels on white cats are white, and the anal fin usually has nineteen to twenty-three rays. Channel cats and blues have dark barbels and more anal fin rays.

Size

Three- to 5-pound white cats are fairly common in some prime waters, but whites exceeding 6 pounds are exceptional in most areas. The largest on record, a truly unusual fish, weighed 22 pounds. That specimen was caught in California, a state where transplanted white cats thrive and often grow very large. In fact, transplanted white catfish often seem to grow much larger in waters where they are not native. Records for states outside the fish's original range, such as Nevada (16 pounds, 15 ounces) and Oregon (15 pounds), often are much heavier than records for states where white cats originally were found.

Range

Before introductions of other species, white catfish were the largest of the native catfishes found in rivers draining into the Atlantic. They ranged from

New York's Hudson River south through Florida. Whites are also native to Gulf of Mexico tributaries in Alabama and Mississippi. They have been transplanted with varied success to ponds, lakes, and rivers in California, Connecticut, Illinois, Indiana, Kentucky, Maine, Massachusetts, Nevada, New Hampshire, Ohio, Oregon, Pennsylvania, Rhode Island, and Washington. Healthy populations often are present in the brackish water of coastal rivers where other cats are absent. The white catfish also is established in several reservoirs in Puerto Rico and has recently been found in Great Britain.

Habitat

White catfish live in channels, pools, and backwaters in rivers, mostly in sluggish current over mud bottoms. They sometimes venture into swift water, but not as much as channel catfish. They also live in lakes and river impoundments.

Of all the catfishes, whites are the most tolerant of saltwater, being found in salinities up to eight parts per million. They live in brackish bays and tidewater sections of many coastal streams.

In habitat preference, white catfish are midway between the channel catfish, which use firmer bottoms and swift currents, and bullheads, which live in slow water over soft, silty bottoms.

Diet

White catfish feed on a wide variety of aquatic animals, including fish (shad, sculpins, sunfish, perch, and others), frogs, insects, clams, crayfish, and crabs. They are scavengers and opportunists as well, sometimes eating plant and animal debris (the feet of a coot were found in one fish) and terrestrial creatures such as slugs, earthworms, small birds and mammals, and even lizards. They also prey on fish eggs and fry and sometimes destroy spawning sites of native fish. Where transplanted, they are believed responsible for declining populations of some native species, including Sacramento perch and trout in portions of California.

Bullheads

In some midwestern states, bullheads, the smallest catfish commonly caught on hook and line, are the number-one ranked fish in terms of

Bullheads don't get very big, but many anglers target them because they are delicious eating.

numbers taken. On light tackle, they're respectable fighters. Rolled in seasoned cornmeal and fried golden-brown, they're favorites on the dinner table.

Many colorful nicknames are used to describe bullheads. "Horned pout" seems universal. It was derived from the fish's sharp pectoral fins, or "horns," and from the European word "pout," which means big-headed fish. The nicknames "greaser" and "slick" also are widely used, and no doubt refer to the gooey slime covering all bullheads. Other colloquial names include polliwog, polly, paperskin, mud cat, stinger, snapper, butterball, bullcat, and bullpout.

Bullheads eat many types of foods, from minnows and crayfish to carrion and insects. "They will take any kind of bait," wrote Henry David Thoreau, "from angleworms to a piece of tomato can . . ."

While using a piece of tomato can for bait might be stretching your luck, there's no denying these nocturnal feeders are not temperamental. My favorite bait is chicken liver. Worms rank a close second. Stinkbaits also are first-rate enticements.

Use light tackle to savor your rock-'em-sock-'em battles with these bantam cats. Four- to 8-pound line is appropriate in all but the most snag-infested waters. Hooks for bullheads range in size from No. 4 to 1/0.

Bullheads feed around the clock, but the night bite usually is best. Zero in on weed-bed edges, river bends, channel drops, underwater humps, inundated ponds, boat docks, and long points.

Water turbidity seems to have little to do with the catch rate. In fact, some very impressive creels are taken from the muddiest water. Bullheads tolerate high levels of turbidity better than most fish, and because they feed primarily by taste and smell, low visibility is not a problem.

As a rule, the simpler your fishing methods, the more you will enjoy bullhead fishing. Your fishing strategy can be as unencumbered as using a cane pole and small hook to dunk a worm or piece of liver. Fish on the bottom, using a small sinker to carry your bait down. Or use a bobber to float the bait just slightly above bottom. You need not fish deep or far from shore.

Three species of bullheads commonly are caught by North American anglers.

Black bullhead. DUANE RAVER, USFWS

Black Bullhead (*Ameiurus melas*)

- Description: The largest bullhead—dark and robust with an almost square or slightly notched tail. Adults are brownish yellow to black but have no mottling. The anal fin has seventeen to twenty-one rays. Gray or black chin barbels are present, but never white. The pectoral fin spines have weakly developed teeth along the rear edge or no teeth at all.

- World record: 8 pounds, 15 ounces.
- Range: From southern Canada, the Great Lakes, and the St. Lawrence River south to the Gulf of Mexico, and from Montana and New Mexico east to the Appalachians.
- Habitat: A common resident of ponds, lakes, streams, and swamps.

Brown Bullhead (*Ameiurus nebulosus*)

- Description: One of the most-sought members of the bullhead clan because of its large average size. In parts of New England, this is the only catfish available to anglers. The sides of brown bullheads usually have a distinct, irregular brownish mottling over a light background. The degree of mottling, however, is highly variable. The belly is creamy white. This species is very similar to the black bullhead, but has well-developed teeth on the rear edges of the pectoral spines (versus no teeth or weakly developed teeth) and twenty-one to twenty-four anal fin rays (versus seventeen to twenty-one). Unlike the yellow bullhead, its chin barbels are pigmented with gray or black.

Brown bullhead. DUANE RAVER, USFWS

- World record: 6 pounds, 2 ounces.
- Range: Throughout the eastern half of the U.S. and into southern Canada. Widely introduced outside its native range.
- Habitat: Prefers moderately clear, heavily vegetated streams and lakes.

Yellow Bullhead (*Ameiurus natalis*)

- Description: The yellow bullhead closely resembles brown and black bullheads, with a squat body and a round or square tail. It differs in having white chin barbels (versus gray or black barbels) and in having twenty-four to twenty-seven anal fin rays (versus fewer than twenty-four anal rays). Adults have a solid yellowish to brownish or black body with no mottling. The belly is white.
- World record: 4 pounds, 8 ounces.

- Range: Widespread, living throughout the eastern and central U.S., with many transplants elsewhere.
- Habitat: Tends to inhabit smaller, weedier bodies of water than its cousins. Common in areas of dense vegetation in shallow, clear bays of lakes, ponds, and slow-moving streams.

Three other bullheads—the flat bullhead, snail bullhead, and spotted bullhead—also swim our waters. Their range is confined to small portions of the southeastern U.S., and none exceeds a foot in length.

Yellow bullhead. DUANE RAVER, USFWS

CHAPTER THREE

Where Monster Cats Live

To catch the catfish of a lifetime, you need to know the special hangouts where these giants live. Some hotspots are readily visible and easily identified; others must be pinpointed using sonar and may be so subtle that they're hard to find. Tag along with a veteran catfisherman and get him to teach you how to zero in on honeyholes or use your own savvy to locate them. When you have identified a dozen or so, you'll have yourself a pattern for finding whopper catfish.

Carry along bottom contour maps of the places you fish and mark hotspots for future reference. Better yet, add waypoints to a GPS unit to accomplish the same end.

Here's another good idea: Take a notepad on every trip and write down a name for each honeyhole where you catch catfish. Use easy-to-remember names that have meaning to you—Car Hole, Lew's Lunker Ledge, Channel Cat Cove, Pat's Point, etc. Thus named, your cat spots will be identified more easily, especially if you fish regularly with a friend who's as crazy as you are about catching cats.

Anglers who consistently catch big catfish know where these giants live and how to find them.

Ten Best River Hangouts

Outside Bends

Rivers follow the path of least resistance. When a hard bottom obstructs the flow, the river changes direction, forming a hard-bottomed outside bend with current. These bends are trophy cat honeyholes, especially for flatheads, which love dark hollows. The river gouges the bank, forming undercuts. The undercut ledge or lip offers natural seclusion to giant cats waiting for a meal.

Erosion topples trees on the bend into the water. This creates an additional hotspot where hungry cats find plentiful forage. If a deepwater pool lies just downstream, productivity increases even more.

Fallen timber in an outside river bend attracts flatheads and other catfish.

When fishing a dam tailrace, target the "grooves" of slower-moving water.

The wing dike in the background produced this huge blue cat.
MATT SUTTON

Tailraces

Catfish congregate in dam tailraces to feed on abundant forage animals. Their numbers increase during the prespawn period when upstream migrations are blocked. During summer, there's another influx of cats moving from oxygen-poor areas downstream to oxygen-rich water below the dam.

Most tailrace anglers fish from shore near the dam. Long upstream casts put the bait into "grooves" of slower-moving water between open gates for a productive drift. Other catters motor to the safe or legal limit from the dam and fish from a boat. Either way, chances are excellent for hooking trophy cats of all species.

Wing Dikes

These narrow rock structures on navigable rivers direct current into the main channel to reduce erosion. Cats gather beside them, with actively feeding fish usually near the river bottom on the dike's upstream side. Water hydraulics here create a "tube" of reduced current running the length of the dike. Hungry cats can hold and feed in this food-rich zone without expending excess energy. Therefore, it pays to focus your efforts on the upstream side.

When targeting big cats, drop a weighted bait into one of the circular whirlpools of water (eddies) near the ends of wing dikes. These are *the* prime feeding sites, so they usually hold larger, more dominant cats.

Underwater Humps and Boulders

Humps and boulders always merit the catfish angler's attention. Unless they rise close to the surface, they are difficult to find without electronic equipment. Those with shallow crowns may be visible or at least apparent due to the boil-line above them.

At night and on cloudy or rainy days, catfish move to the shallowest part of humps, feeding on baitfish attracted to the structure. This is a great place to fish on hot summer nights. When fishing is confined to daylight hours, look for cats positioned on shaded portions of the hump or around deepwater edges where light penetration is minimal.

Fish boulders as you would a wing dike. Most feeding cats are near bottom on the upstream edge, with a few feeding near the crown and boil-line areas. Cats in slack water behind boulders are usually inactive.

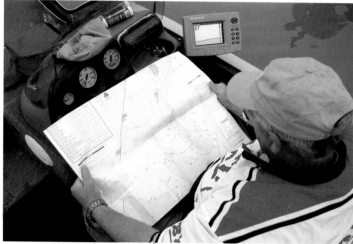

A bottom contour map and sonar fish-finder can help pinpoint underwater catfish structure such as humps and holes.

Holes

Although sometimes difficult to pinpoint, river-bottom holes are big-cat magnets. These structures break current, providing resting and feeding spots for blues, channels, and flatheads. In smaller rivers, holes form below shoals where current washes away bottom substrate. In big rivers, look for holes directly below dams, near outside bends, and near tributary mouths. Sonar helps identify this structure.

Cats holed up often remain motionless, waiting for food to drift nearby. Consequently, baits must pass close to elicit strikes. Work holes thoroughly, top to bottom, front to back, and note where strikes occur. Concentrate on the most productive spots.

Cats stay in deeper areas during sunny days, moving to shallow spots to feed at night and on cloudy days. Place your bait accordingly.

Tributary Mouths

Tributary mouths are staging areas for prespawn and postspawn catfish. If the mouth is relatively deep, or if the tributary channel joins a primary creek or river channel on the bottom, the area may have good trophy potential year-round. During cool months, tributaries with a warm inflow attract the most catfish. Cool creeks are best during summer. Heavy rains that wash food animals into the main water body also draw cats to mouths of feeder creeks and rivers.

Tributaries of large rivers draw spawning cats and fish looking for more comfortable water temperatures.

Catfish usually ambush prey from behind current breaks—humps, holes, or trees—near the confluence of the tributary within the main river or lake. Cast your rig upstream and allow it to drift past these honeyholes.

Drift Piles

These mats of floating logs and debris form in backwaters of big rivers during high water. As current velocity and wave action increase, moving water presses against the seam of still backwater, causing it to circulate like a giant vortex. Logs sucked into this eddy often form huge drifts, or rafts. The drifts attract baitfish and other forage, which in turn attract catfish.

Drift piles are difficult to fish but often harbor numerous catfish.

The best way to fish drift piles is to let the current carry bait under the outer edges. Fish the enticement on an egg-sinker or slip float rig.

Bars

Rock, gravel, and sandbars—common in most rivers—are good catfishing areas when water is high and current strong. For this reason, it pays to learn the location of bars when low water exposes them.

With the water low, it's easy to see current-breaking areas on this sandbar where feeding cats might lurk when the river is at a normal level.

Catfish gather around bars to avoid excessive current and are especially common here when concentrations of forage animals are available. In the lower Mississippi River, for instance, thousands of small leeches "hatch" from sandbars in late summer, attracting enormous schools of channel catfish. Rock and gravel bars on the lower Arkansas River in Arkansas harbor dense populations of crayfish when spring's high water begins to recede. Catfish of all sorts gather to feed on this seasonal banquet.

As the water level falls, the tops of bars may be exposed. When this happens, catfish and forage animals move to deeper sections of the bar, usually near the channel end. Adjust your fishing tactics accordingly.

Chutes

Deepwater chutes are overlooked by many catfish hunters but often hold heavy concentrations of actively feeding, trophy-class catfish. Chutes occur where a river narrows, sometimes splitting to go around an island or other midstream obstruction. Cats tend to gather near the upstream and downstream edges of the chute where current slackens, especially if gravel bars or other current breaks are present.

For the best results, move to one end of the chute and release line a few feet at a time, allowing the bait to drift near bottom. Stop the bait occasionally and allow it to remain stationary a few moments. If no pick-ups occur, release more line and repeat the process. Give the bait plenty of time to tempt fish and watch for suddenly slack line, which indicates a taker.

Bridges

In summer, catfish frequently hold near bridge pilings. This is an area of cool, shady, well-oxygenated water where aquatic invertebrates and baitfish are found in abundance. Where food and comfort are found, catfish lurk.

With sonar, you can ease along the pilings and determine the depth and position of fish concentrations. Catfish frequently are suspended at mid-depths. Find them, then back your boat away from the bridge and cast a slightly weighted bait past a piling, letting it drift down while you count. If a cat is caught, count down to the same level on your next cast.

After fishing pilings, work riprap lining the adjacent shore. Cast parallel to the bank, starting fairly deep and gradually working deeper as you move away from the bank. Live crayfish and baitfish work great in this situation.

Ten Best Lake Hangouts

Bottom Channels and Ditches

Some lakes have prominent bottom channels; others have subtle ditches and drops. All such structures are trophy cat magnets you can find with sonar.

Main channels act like major highways, leading migrating catfish from one part of the water body to another. Small branches act as secondary roads, leading migratory fish toward shallow-water habitat. Big catfish especially like channel junctions.

Trophy cats usually stay near deep water falling into the channel. Look for them near features on the ledge that distinguish it from surrounding areas—brushpiles, points, adjacent humps, cuts in the bank, etc.

During the day, anchor in the shallowest water near the dropoff and fish deeper water. At night, do the opposite to catch cats moving shallow to feed.

A drawdown has exposed primary and secondary bottom channels in this lake, ideal structure for catfish.

Riprap

Engineers often place riprap (large rocks along shorelines to prevent erosion) near dams, bridges, and causeways on lakes, and on many rivers as well. Riprap appeals to catfish because it attracts forage animals and provides cover, depth, and shade. Large channel cats and flatheads, especially, like this habitat.

When fishing a long, look-alike stretch of riprap, focus on objects distinguishing a small section. A pipe or fallen tree may attract catfish. Other times, a difference in the rocks does the trick. Watch for big boulders changing to smaller rocks or slides of rocks creating points.

Inundated Lakes and Ponds

Small ponds and lakes inundated when larger lakes fill are prime locales for trophy cats of all species. These offer easy access to deepwater holding areas and shallow feeding spots. They're especially productive in large, shallow lakes.

Pinpoint a spot with sonar, and then look within it for points, drop-offs, sunken islands, or humps that may attract cats. If scattered trees or stumps exist around the perimeter, fish them carefully.

Riprap is like a magnet for catfish, providing food, shelter, and depth.

Windswept Shores

Heavy wind produces a chain reaction on fertile lakes. The wind blows floating plankton (microscopic plants and animals) against the shore. Minnows, shad, and other baitfish that feed on plankton follow their food to shoreline reaches. Catfish that feed on baitfish follow, too. For this reason, fishing shorelines pounded by heavy winds often produces extraordinary catches of catfish. It's a situation every catfish angler should exploit.

Docks

Boat docks often attract big cats. The best, on wood pilings in 5 to 15 feet of water near cover and/or structure, have been in the water several seasons and are close to the surface. Docks meeting these criteria attract catfish by providing shade throughout the day. The pilings offer a sense of security, which structure-oriented catfish require, and also harbor a smorgasbord of foods. Algae growing on the seasoned wood attract small invertebrates, which in turn attract baitfish that draw in big cats.

Catfish often feed beneath big, low-lying docks like this.

Size is another consideration. Think of docks as catfish hotels. Big hotels have rooms for lots of guests. Occupancy is limited at smaller establishments. If other traits are equal, concentrate on large docks.

Move in close and fish under docks. Rig with heavy line, because fighting cats can break you off quick on pilings and other structure.

Humps

For the cat fan, locating an underwater hump, rise, or submerged island is like finding a map to buried treasure. These structures are among the most productive catfishing spots in any lake, especially during summer.

When you've pinpointed a hump with sonar, learn all you can about it—size, the steepness of drops on each side, existing cover, and so forth. Narrow your fishing area to a few choice zones—points, pockets, rock beds, timbered or brushy areas, etc.—and mark them with buoys.

Note the depth of the hump below the surface. Humps rising no closer than 40 or 50 feet of the surface may be below the thermocline, with oxygen levels too low to support catfish. The best humps are 5 to 20 feet from the surface and have substantial deep water around them, such as a creek channel running alongside. Humps with timber, brush, rocks, or other cover are also very productive.

When rains raise the water level in this lake, this hump will be a prime hotspot for big catfish.

Fishing discharge areas of lakeside power plants can often lead to extraordinary catches of big catfish.

Many catfish anglers bypass dense beds of aquatic vegetation, preferring instead to fish in less bothersome places. But weed beds often harbor nice catfish.

Power Plants

Facilities for generating electricity are a common sight on many large lakes. Water flowing into the power plant and then out creates a subsurface current covering a big area in a lake, and large numbers of catfish often hold near the mouths of discharge and inlet channels and out into the lake where there's still a hint of moving water.

Sometimes the current hugs the shore; in other lakes, it may curve out into the main lake. When you figure out the current pattern, you can fish places where you have a better chance of locating catfish. Hot-water discharges are especially attractive to catfish in cooler months.

Weed Beds and Thickets

Weed beds and brushy thickets provide first-rate action for savvy catters. Most anglers assume the interior of these hotspots can't be fished and confine their fishing to the edges. They may miss big cats hiding deep in the cover.

The trick to catching these cats is working methodically to cover every accessible nook and pocket. A heavy jigging pole is tops for this because it allows you to reach likely honeyholes from a distance with fewer hang-ups. Attach a float above your bait, and probe every opening you see, changing the float's position until you determine the depth where fish are feeding.

Don't be shy about fishing tiny, impossible looking openings. Chances are, your bait will penetrate quite easily, and catfish in such places are far more likely to strike than those found on edges pounded by every passing angler.

Creeks and Rivers

The area where a creek or river empties into a lake can be a honeyhole when conditions are right. Catfishing is outstanding after rains when high flow carries forage into the reservoir. In early spring, an incoming creek or shallow stream may bring warmer water that attracts baitfish and, consequently, catfish. Cool- or cold-water stream mouths have excellent potential in summer, especially at night.

Oxbow Run-outs

If you fish for catfish in big river-bottom oxbow lakes, learn all you can about a phenomenon known as "the run-off." This occurs when a river "falls out of" a connected oxbow, usually in spring or early summer when overflow waters recede from the river bottoms. There comes a point, when the water has fallen low enough, that the only connections between an oxbow and its parent stream are small "run-outs" created by low points in the topography. Sometimes only one run-out exists; occasionally, there are several. All run-outs serve up extraordinary catfishing.

Water constricted in run-outs is swift, and forage animals are pulled by current into the rushing stream of water and adjacent areas. Catfish gather to gorge on the resulting feast. Some hold near cover at the head of the run-out, in the lake. Others position themselves at the run-out's tail, where the rushing water meets the river. All feed ravenously, and any bait—night crawlers, cut-bait, live fish, crayfish—drifted through or along the run-out area is likely to be taken.

The run-out area between an oxbow lake and the adjoining river can be a honeyhole for catfish when conditions are right.

Five Best Pond Hangouts

Deep Holes

Pond catfish (typically channel cats and/or bullheads) often stay in the deepest water, usually close to the levee or dam if one is present. They may

The author caught these winter channel cats in a deep hole in a friend's pond. ALEX HINSON

leave the depths to feed in shallows, but they always return. Cats abandon holes only when oxygen levels fall too low, such as when a pond stratifies in summer.

Deep holes are particularly good during daylight hours when cats seek the sanctuary of darkness. Fishing here may produce fish in spring, summer, and autumn, but winter months outshine others. During this season, cats pile up in cold-water congregations where a single school may contain hundreds of fish.

Fish vertically beneath a boat if possible. Use a weight and hook only, with chicken liver or night crawlers for bait. Freespool the bait to the bottom, reel up a foot or so, then get ready for action.

Creek Coves

Creek coves, where feeder creeks enter a pond, are good places during spring and early autumn when catfish are ready to invade the shallows. Inflowing creek water also provides relief from extreme summer and winter temperatures. Water coming into the pond is usually much cooler or warmer than the pond itself.

Look for catfish hanging right on the creek channel's edge. The channel usually runs through the cove and passes somewhere through the cove mouth. For thorough coverage, fish both sides of the cove mouth carefully, trying to locate catfish along the dropoff the channel creates. Then move back into the cove and fish the spot where the creek enters the pond by fanning a series of casts to cover the entire area.

Aquatic Vegetation

Vegetation also should get your attention in ponds. Plant cover not only provides food, comfort, and safety for catfish, it also can indicate a pond's bottom structure. For example, weed growth commencing along the shoreline and extending out 30 or 40 feet indicates a shallow flat. The bottom may drop sharply on the weed line's outer edge, something you should check.

Look for islands of weeds separate from the distinct contour of the shoreline, as these are exceptional catfish attractors. Watch, too, for openings in weed beds where you can drop in a bait. Catfish love these cool, food-rich confines, and any natural bait presented here is likely to be devoured. Any changes in contour (pockets or indentations) along weed edges also should be investigated.

Woody Cover

In sizing up a pond, also look for woody cover such as stumps, dead snags, logs washed up against the shore, and trees toppled along the bank. Catfish often feed adjacent to these objects, in both shallow and deep water. Drop a baited hook right next to the wood and you're liable to pull out a big ol' cat.

Water-Control Structures

Many ponds have water-control structures that bring an inflow of fresh water. This may be a pipe jutting from a bank with water pouring out the end, an underwater well head that creates a boil in an otherwise calm surface, or a big culvert

The outer edge of a weed bed often indicates a sharp drop where catfish feed.

Catfish frequently gather near water-control structures that bring cooler, more oxygenated water into a pond.

with a fresh inflow of rain after a shower. Baitfish gather in the well-oxygenated water around these structures, and catfish gather to eat the baitfish. Allowing a bait to drift through the area beneath a float is one good way to catch these often-scattered cats.

CHAPTER FOUR

What Makes Catfish Bite?

I've had many interesting conversations with people who possess great knowledge of catfish. Scores of guides and friends have shared their fishing secrets, and dozens of biologists have taught me about the life histories of blues, channel cats, flatheads, and other species. One conversation in particular proved to be an eye-opener for me. In fact, the things I learned during that talk were so amazing and so important to me as an angler that I feel it is important to share that discussion here.

The person with whom I had that talk is Dr. John T. Caprio, a neurophysiologist at Louisiana State University in Baton Rouge. Since 1971, he's been studying the senses of catfish, particularly the senses of taste and smell and how they relate to the feeding behavior of catfish. The facts he shared heightened my already great appreciation for these often misunderstood and underrated sportfish and have made me a much better fisherman. They'll prove useful to you as well.

Taste

I'll never forget the first thing Dr. Caprio told me about catfish.

"Catfish are swimming tongues," he said. "These are scaleless animals, and their whole body is taste buds from head to tail. To use an analogy, it's as if the tip of your tongue grew out and covered your body."

A catfish just 6 inches long, he noted, has more than 250,000 taste buds on its body. On a giant blue cat or flathead, the taste buds number in the many millions. Each square centimeter of skin has at least 5,000 taste buds.

"In humans, taste buds are found only in the mouth—on the tongue, the palate, and so forth—and they're not that dense," Caprio said. "A catfish, on the other hand, has huge concentrations of taste buds, not just in the mouth but everywhere. The densest concentrations are on the gill rakers, so the fish can taste things in the water as it flows over the gills. But taste buds cover the outside of the catfish as well—the whiskers, fins, back, belly, sides, and even the tail. The whiskers, in particular, have lots of taste buds. Under a microscope, each whisker, or barbel, looks like a field

Every inch of skin on a catfish's body is covered with taste buds that help the fish locate food.

of volcanoes. Every volcano is a taste bud. So the idea that the catfish is a swimming tongue is a perfectly reasonable statement.

"If you were a catfish," Caprio told me, "you could taste a slice of pepperoni pizza just by sitting on it."

Smell

According to Caprio, the catfish's olfactory sense is keen as well.

"The catfish's sense of smell and the taste system, in terms of sensitivity, are about the same," he said. "They can smell and taste some compounds at one part to ten billion parts of water. That's how acute their senses are."

Water flows over folds of sensitive tissue inside the catfish's nostrils, allowing the fish to detect certain substances in its environment. The number of these folds seems related to sharpness of smell. Channel cats have more than 140. Rainbow trout have only eighteen, largemouth bass eight to thirteen.

Because the sense of smell is so important to catfish, many anglers believe smelly baits are the best to use, but Caprio disputed this contention.

All catfish have paired nostrils between the eye and the mouth. Water goes in one nostril and out the other, passing over sensitive odor-detecting tissue.

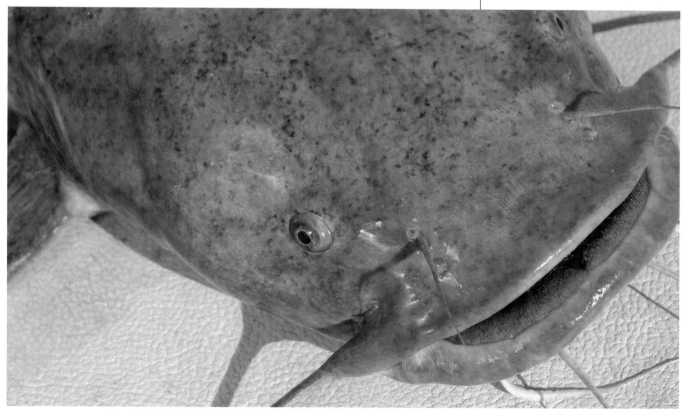

"Most anglers think horrible smelling baits work best," he told me. "But that's crazy. What stinks to you and me doesn't stink to fish. We're smelling chemicals volatilized to the air, but animals living in water can't detect volatiles. They detect chemical compounds in the water instead. What you and I smell, fish can't smell, so how terrible a bait smells or doesn't smell to us has no bearing at all on whether or not a catfish will eat it."

Hearing

With no visible ears, it might seem that catfish can't hear well, but that's not true.

"A catfish's body is the same density as water, so it doesn't need external ears," Caprio said. "Sound waves traveling through water go right through a catfish. When sound waves hit the fish's swim bladder, the bladder starts vibrating. This amplifies sound waves, which then travel to small bones called otoliths in the inner ear. The otoliths start vibrating, too, and as they vibrate, they bend little hairlike projections on the cells beneath them. Nerves in these cells carry a sound message to the brain."

The swim bladder on most fish is independent of the inner ear. But in catfish, a series of bones called the Weberian ossicles connect the swim bladder and inner ear. Fish without these bone connections (bass and trout, for instance) can detect sounds from about 20 to 1,000 cycles per second. Catfish can hear sounds of much higher frequency, up to about 13,000 cycles per second.

Lateral Line

Low-frequency sounds undetectable by the catfish's inner ear are picked up by the lateral line, a series of little pores along the fish's sides. Inside the pores are cells with hairlike projections. These projections bend in response to water displacements, thus stimulating nerve endings that signal the brain. The catfish uses this system to locate nearby prey, potential enemies, and other catfish. Creatures scurrying across the bottom, flopping at the surface, swimming through the water, or walking along the shore all create low-frequency vibrations that the lateral line detects.

The lateral line helps a catfish detect vibrations and low-frequency sounds.

"This 'vibrational' sense is very well developed in catfish," Caprio noted. "One interesting point relating to this is the fact that the Chinese have used catfish for centuries to warn of earthquakes. Catfish can detect a lot of earthquakes days in advance because they have an ultra-sensitivity to low-frequency vibrations."

Eyesight

Catfish also have an excellent sense of sight.

"Channel catfish, in particular, have great eyesight," said Caprio. "In fact, the eye of the channel catfish is used in many medical centers for vision research."

Caprio pointed out that catfish in clear water often will strike fishing lures, with no sensory cues other than sight triggering this action. They see something that looks like prey, and they attack.

Cones in the eyes indicate catfish have color vision. This is borne out by the experiments of some anglers. In his book *Catfishing*, Chris Altman

Although the eyes of catfish are relatively small, they provide keen sight for zeroing in on prey in water that's not too turbid.

wrote about one angler who places half-inch sections of plastic worms on his hooks along with his baits, primarily to provide a splash of color. "The piece of plastic worm makes the bait a bit more buoyant," the angler told Altman, "but I believe it functions most effectively as an attractor to the catfish, something to get the fish's attention. We have done informal studies on the technique and, invariably, the angler using the piece of plastic gets a bite more often."

Catfish eyes also have structures that enhance their night-feeding abilities. Rods improve dim-light sight, and each eye is lined with a layer of crystals (the tapetum lucidum) that reflects gathered light on the retina, thus improving the fish's lowlight vision even more. No doubt these ocular enhancements aid shallow-water sight feeding during twilight hours.

Touch

A lack of scales heightens the catfish's sense of touch as well. Their smooth skin is very sensitive, and the brush of wiry fishing line or something else out of place in their environment may send them scurrying.

Electroreception

Most extraordinary of all, perhaps, is a sense called electroreception. Catfish don't have to see prey or smell it or taste it. Tiny clusters of special cells on the head and along the lateral line detect electrical fields in living organisms. A catfish can find its prey through electroreception, just like sharks.

"A catfish has electroreceptors all over its head," says Caprio. "These little pores work because every living cell is a battery. That is, if you stick an electrode inside a cell and outside a cell, you get some kind of reading just as if you were measuring a battery with a voltmeter. So, catfish use the electric sense to help them find food. It's a very close sense. They must be within inches of the object. Catfish can dig in the mud and find insect larvae, worms, and such by using their electric sense alone."

Anatomy of the Bite

All the senses interact when a catfish seeks something to eat. The sensory organs detect chemicals, vibrations, and/or electric charges from potential food items and send messages to the fish's brain telling it to find the food. Then, when the cat picks up the food, taste buds relay messages to another part of the brain and tell it to eat the food—or spit it out.

"All the catfish's senses are used," says Caprio. "It's like you or me going to a restaurant. You walk in. The food looks and smells good, so you order a steak. The waiter brings it on a covered platter; it smells great. You really want this steak, but when the waiter lifts the top, the steak is blue. Now you don't want it.

"You see, many sensory cues control your feeding behavior. The same thing is true with fish. A catfish doesn't just search with its nose or taste buds or eyes. It uses every sensory cue available before deciding to eat."

All the catfish's senses work together to tell it when to eat prey, or an angler's bait.

Sensory Turnoffs

If a catfish tastes or smells certain compounds in the water or on your bait, feeding activities may cease. These compounds include such things as gasoline, and certain ingredients in sunscreen, tobacco, insect repellent, and other items commonly used by fishermen. You'll catch more cats if you avoid contact with such materials as much as possible.

Vision, however, is the sense most likely to cause fright in a catfish, according to Caprio.

"If a bird flies overhead, or someone casts a shadow that moves across the water, all feeding may cease," he says. "We have fouled up lab experiments for weeks just by having someone put their hand over the top of a tank. If you tape the silhouette of a bird predator to the top of a fish's tank, that cat won't come out to eat, no matter how hungry it gets. The fish will die before he goes out and gets food right in front of it, unless you turn the lights off. Then he'll come out immediately and feed. That's one reason many catfishermen are more successful when fishing at night. No shadows."

The exceptionally powerful senses of catfish allow them to thrive in a wide variety of habitats. They cope better than other fish in difficult environments, and thus are often found where other fish are not. The next time you hook a big one, think about how it found your bait. It will help you better appreciate the remarkable senses of these extraordinary fish.

CHAPTER FIVE

Tackle Tips

Catfishermen probably use a wider variety of tackle than any other group of anglers. Take rods, for example. Cat aficionados employ everything from tiny spinning rods to super-long surf-casting rods.

If you spend most of your time dabbling for bullheads in farm ponds, an ultralight spinning outfit works great. If channel cats are your quarry, a 6-foot, medium-action bass-fishing combo may satisfy. If you want to catch a trophy blue or flathead, you may want to go equipped with a 10- to 16-foot saltwater baitcasting rig constructed with the sturdiest materials.

Options are equally diverse for other types of gear, but don't let yourself get overwhelmed by the variety available. Selecting the right tackle is common sense shopping, really. Check out the selections and study the information that follows, then buy the best tackle you can afford for the conditions and catfish you usually encounter.

Rods and Reels

Rods 7 feet or longer offer several advantages over short rods when catfishing. Casting distance increases with a longer rod, important if you're bankfishing or angling in clear water. Long rods give more "reach," so you can work rigs properly around cover or keep a cat out of your prop. Long rods let you hold more line out of the water, allowing quicker hooksets and better bait control and permitting more accurate drifts and natural presentation when stream fishing. Long rods also provide more leverage for battling heavyweight cats.

Fiberglass, graphite, and combinations of these are the most popular materials for rods. Fiberglass is more durable than graphite but lacks graphite's sensitivity. Graphite is lighter and stiffer. Fiberglass is heavier and bends more easily with the same amount of pull. Graphite is much more expensive than fiberglass, another consideration.

Fiberglass/graphite composites offer the best of both worlds—strength, sensitivity, flexibility, and moderate pricing. They probably are the best choice for most cat fans. Also consider E-glass rods. They're super-tough, with extra strength for lifting, pulling, and casting heavy rigs.

A rod's action—the flexibility or stiffness it exhibits—also can be important.

Fast Action: This style bends very little; in fact, only the tip section will actually bend. This is ideal for targeting big, heavy catfish.

Medium Action: A medium-action rod is the most common choice when the angler will be using various applications for a variety of species. These rods bend for about half their length, allowing an angler to fish for small and large species with good control and hooksetting allowances.

Slow Action: A slow-action rod bends throughout nearly its whole length, providing the most flexible action available. These rods are used almost exclusively for panfish such as bullheads, allowing a better fight for the angler.

Keep these points in mind about rod components as well:

- Long, reinforced fighting butts and blank-through-handle construction provide superior strength and leverage for big-cat battles.
- White and light-colored models are easier to see at night.

- Rods with glow-in-the-dark tips are helpful for detecting night bites.
- EVA foam handles are more durable than cork.
- Poor-quality line guides and rod tips can wear out or break. One-piece, double-wrapped, double-footed, stainless-steel models perform best.

Baitcasting reels are more durable than other types (spinning and spincast) and provide more fish-cranking power. Look for a solid frame, tough gears, and smooth casting, plus adequate line capacity. The best models hold at least 200 yards of 17- to 20-pound monofilament.

The best baitcasters have a "clicker" mechanism. This produces an audible signal when line is pulled from the reel, thus indicating a catfish bite. The clicker also keeps a soft, steady tension on the spool, which prevents backlashes when a cat runs with a bait.

Spinning reels don't offer the cranking power or line-pickup speed baitcasters provide. Their primary application is when fishing light line (anything less than 12- to 14-pound-test). They allow greater casting distance when using light baits, and they're also good for landing fish on light line because there is significantly less friction caused by the guides, which are on the underside of the blank. Especially good are spinning reels with a drag system that allows you to fish with the bail closed for more security and control. When a lever is engaged, the reel goes to a tension-controlled freespool that allows cats to take bait without feeling resistance. Turning the reel handle disengages the feature, allowing a quick hookset as you prepare to reel the fish in.

Spincast reels are still the traditional favorites of many catfish fans. None has the winching power or line capacity of a large baitcaster, but each offers simple push-button casting control with a soft delivery suitable for stinkbaits and small natural baits. This type of reel is perfect for children learning to cast, but don't expect one to hold up well when battling a trophy-class catfish.

Fishing Line

Line is arguably the most important equipment item for catfish anglers. It plays a key role in bait presentation and in hooking and landing fish. Yet many anglers remain confused and uneducated about line types and the special properties each exhibits. Studying these facts can help.

Monofilament. Monofilament lines are the most popular, accounting for more than two-thirds of all fishing lines sold. As the name suggests, this is a single-component product. It is created through an extrusion process in which molten plastic is formed into a strand through a die. This process is relatively inexpensive, producing a less costly product—that being the main reason monos are so popular. It's important to remember, however, that cheaper brands of monofilament usually don't receive the quality-control attention, additives, and attention in the finishing process that premium-grade lines receive. As a result, they may not offer the superb blend of tensile strength, limpness, abrasion resistance, and knot strength that are characteristic of more expensive monos. In other words, you get what you pay for. If you use monofilament, test several name brands and stick with those you know and trust.

Braids. Before the discovery of nylon, braided Dacron was the most popular line. Dacron possessed poor knot strength, low abrasion resistance, and little stretch, however, so it was used much less after superior monofilaments were introduced in the 1950s. Today, it maintains only a very small niche in the marketplace, being used primarily by some catfishermen who believe its softness improves their catch rate.

In the early 1990s, gel-spun and aramid fibers such as Spectra, Kevlar, and Dyneema entered the fishing-line market, creating a new category of braided lines often called "superlines" or "microfilaments." These synthetic fibers are thin and incredibly strong (more than ten times stronger than steel). Individual fiber strands are joined through an intricate braiding process to produce ultra thin, super strong, very sensitive, yet also somewhat expensive lines.

Because it's smaller in diameter, superline is less visible than monofilament, and anglers can spool more line on their reels. Superlines have little stretch, transmitting strikes instantly to the rod tip, thus providing more positive hooksets. Plus, superlines allow longer casts, making them ideal for bankfishermen. High break strength and low stretch permit better manhandling of big catfish.

Superlines require a Palomar knot for best results. (Instructions for tying the Palomar usually are included in the line box.) Put mono backing on your reel before spooling superlines to prevent "slipping" on the reel and to conserve line. This also adds firmness to the spool for better casting and less backlashes. Tie a Uni knot to connect to the mono.

Do not overfill reels with superline. Overfilling creates loose strands after a cast and more backlashes. Fill to ⅛ inch from the spool rim.

A more recent innovation is fused line, made by fusing, rather than braiding, the gel-spun fibers. This process produces what appears to be a single-strand line that is also ultra thin, super strong, and very sensitive. These lines are larger in diameter and offer a bit less strength than original braids, but they are somewhat easier to cast and tie, and generally more affordable.

Fluorocarbon. Fluorocarbon is a polymer that is nearly invisible in water. It is inert, so it resists deterioration by sunlight, gasoline, battery acid, or insect repellents. And it doesn't absorb water.

Fluorocarbon fishing leaders originated in Japan, where anglers are particularly fussy about bait presentations. Japanese fisheries receive heavy pressure, so lifelike bait presentations are important. Nearly invisible fluorocarbon lines enhanced this quality.

Ultimately, U.S. anglers began using fluorocarbon leaders for the same reason—low visibility. It caught on when anglers reported catching more fish with it. The original fluorocarbon leaders were stiff and very expensive, but new technologies have produced more flexible fluorocarbon at more affordable prices.

Fluorocarbon certainly offers advantages in clear-water situations where catfish are heavily pressured or slow to bite. Also, because fluorocarbon does not absorb water, it won't weaken or increase in stretch like mono line. Added density makes fluorocarbon very abrasion resistant, so it's ideal for rough conditions, and makes it sink faster than mono, so baits sink deeper quicker. And because fluorocarbon stretches less than mono and more slowly, it's much more sensitive.

Fluorocarbon lines, like superlines, require special attention. The Trilene knot is the best to use. Make all five wraps when tying the knot, and wet the line before cinching it up to prevent line weakening. Always test the knot before fishing.

All fluorocarbons are still stiffer than nylon, even when wet. This requires more attentiveness to the line when casting, and finer "balance" of tackle. If heavier fluorocarbon line is used on lighter rods, reels, and baits, anglers will experience more difficulty. Baitcasting reels may require additional adjustment for the extra momentum created by the heavier weight of fluorocarbon. Adjust mechanical brakes to the weight of the line and bait to maximize casting distance and minimize overruns.

Terminal Tackle

Every catfish angler carries different items of terminal tackle and paraphernalia that suit his or her particular needs. Some folks I know prefer the simplest options—nothing more than a little tackle box or bag in which to carry a Spartan selection of hooks, sinkers, floats, and other must-have items. Others I know haul half a dozen tackle boxes every time they fish, each stuffed with a different class of tackle that may or may not be needed on a particular day. One box may brim with an assortment of stinkbait worms, stirring paddles, beads, swivels, and other paraphernalia useful for fishing stinkbaits. Another may contain nothing more than sinkers. Yet another may be full of terminal tackle items such as floats, hooks, swivels, and pre-tied rigs. Most anglers fall somewhere between these two extremes, carrying a single tackle box or bag, often large, that will accommodate all the gear needed for a one-day outing.

Here's some advice for selecting and stuffing a tackle box of that sort that's ideal for catfishing.

Hooks

There are two primary considerations when selecting hooks for catfishing—size and style.

Always use the smallest hook that is feasible. Small hooks penetrate quicker than big hooks. And they allow better bait presentations. Small does not mean thin, however. The thin-wire hooks often used by panfishermen will straighten when connected to even a modest-size catfish. Use heavy-gauge designs sturdy enough to hold the fish you're targeting.

Match the size of the hook to the type and size of bait. Bear in mind that the hook point should remain well exposed after impaling the bait. A hook that is too small may set back into the bait on the hookset, failing to make the desired connection.

When fishing small baits for small catfish, you may need nothing larger than a No. 2 to No. 1 hook. A 1/0 or 2/0 hook is good when presenting a small strip of thin cut-bait, but a 3/0 or 4/0 may be required when cut-bait is prepared in thick chunks. A 5/0 or 6/0 is necessary when using bluegills and other live baitfish up to 6 inches. Switch to even larger hooks when using larger baits.

CATFISHING ACCESSORIES

Catfishermen actually need little in the way of tackle and accessories. Need and want are different things, however. You'll certainly want a variety of accessories to make your catfishing junkets more comfortable and productive. Here are some to consider.

- Sonar fish-finder unit to see underwater structure and cover where catfish lurk, and to pinpoint the catfish themselves.

- A GPS unit helps you find your way back to honeyholes.

- Landing net. If you're after trophy cats, always carry a big sturdy landing net with a large reinforced hoop, long handle (at least 48 inches), and a long net (48 inches or more) made from soft small-mesh netting.

- Rod holders for your boat and for bankfishing.

- Fisherman's multitool to remove hooks, cut line, and perform dozens of other tasks.

- Bait gear such as cast nets to catch shad and herring baits and aerated tanks to keep the baitfish alive.

- Cutting board and fillet knives for preparing cut-bait and dressing catfish.

- Skinning pliers. Stainless steel with nonslip handles is best.

- Marker buoys to delineate underwater structure.

- Lanterns and lantern accessories for night fishing.

- Anchor(s) for your boat.

- Spotlight for boating and fishing at night.

- Life jackets are absolutely imperative.

- Drift sock(s) to control the speed of your movement when drift-fishing.

- Bottom contour maps of your favorite fishing lakes.

- A rainsuit.

- Hook hone.

- Fishing towel.

- Emergency rod-tip repair kit.

- Sheer pins and other spare parts for your motor.

- Small flashlight, signal flares, and waterproof matches.

Most catfishermen carry several hook designs in their tackle box. Styles often used for live-bait and cut-bait fishing include Sproat, O'Shaughnessy, Round Bend or Viking, Faultless, Kirby, Kahle, and Octopus. The O'Shaughnessy, an old-time favorite of many catters, is an excellent, sturdy, multipurpose hook available in sizes up to 10/0. The Kahle hook is another favorite. Its wide-gap design provides plenty of room for a large live or cut-bait.

Another style, the circle hook, is popular with catfish anglers. Circle hooks are designed to quickly penetrate a cat's mouth as it struggles against the line. Most cats get hooked in the corner of the mouth, not deep in the gullet. For this reason, cats are more likely to stay hooked and can be released with little or no harm.

Sinkers

Sinkers serve primarily to carry bait down to a water level where catfish are feeding. Choice depends on the type of rig being fished, water depth, current velocity, and bottom conditions. Use a size that has just enough weight to keep your bait in place at the desired level in the water column.

Slip sinkers slide freely on your line, usually above a barrel swivel or split shot used as a stop. Common examples include egg sinkers, bullet sinkers, and walking sinkers.

Other sinker designs commonly used by cat men include bell (also called bass-casting or dipsey sinkers), bank, pyramid, and bottom-bouncer sinkers.

Split shot are versatile and convenient for light-tackle fishing when you need small amounts of weight. They also are used to balance slip floats, weight drift rigs, and as makeshift sinker stops on bottom rigs.

Floats

When selecting floats, take into account the size of the bait and the depth of the fish. Use only those that properly support the bait while being easy to see. Keep several different styles and sizes in your tackle box to match different fishing conditions and rigs.

Fishermen use two basic types of floats—fixed floats, which attach firmly to the line with pegs or spring-loaded hooks, and sliding, or slip, floats that move freely along the line.

Fixed floats are best suited for fishing waters no deeper than the length of your rod. This style of float allows the bait to remain at a preset depth after casting.

In deeper water, or when casting long distances, use a sliding float to eliminate casting problems caused by the long length of line between the float and the hook. These floats slide up and down the line, and your entire rigging (float, sinker, and hook) can be reeled almost to the rod tip. When cast, the float stays on the surface while the sinker pulls the line through the float. A bobber stop or stop knot placed on the line stops line movement and suspends the bait at the preferred depth.

Bright, fluorescent colors stand out on rippled water surfaces much better than white or cork-colored floats. If you're fishing clear, shallow water, or if fish seem fussy, you may want to use a transparent plastic float.

Night floats and European-style floats are also available. Night floats have a small light on top that's powered by a cyalume stick or tiny lithium battery. They're super when catfishing after dark.

European-style floats, most made of balsa, come in numerous styles designed to be used under a wide variety of fishing conditions. They have a thin white line below a brightly colored tip, and floats weighted with split shot down to this "waterline" show even the slightest bite. In still water, for example, the biggest fish often pick up the bait so the bobber rises in the water rather than sinking. This kind of take cannot be seen with typical American floats.

Float shape determines function. "Fat" bobbers float more shot where you need longer casts or where current is strong—on tailwaters, for example. "Antenna" floats with elongated tops work best in still or slowly moving water and with lighter baits. When a fish takes with antennas, you can see where it moves by the tilt of the antenna top and set the hook with a gentle side sweep of your rod.

Several other designs are available for use in differing conditions. Among these are some of the most sensitive fishing floats ever devised, and every catfish angler would be wise to investigate their applications and availability.

Swivels

Hook a catfish, and it's going to twist and roll in the water. So do many of the live baits used by catfish anglers. That's why many anglers add a swivel to their rigs. Swivels also serve as "stops" between slip sinkers and hooks.

Always use quality ball-bearing swivels instead of cheap, brass snap swivels. Three-way swivels are an integral part of some catfish rigs, so keep a batch of those on hand as well.

CHAPTER SIX

The Right Rigs

Using the right fishing rig allows you to target catfish properly regardless of species, the bait you're using, or the type of water you choose to fish. The simplest rig, one that works well in a surprising variety of catfishing situations, is nothing more than a baited hook at the end of your line. But often you'll need a sinker to get your line on or near bottom where catfish usually feed, and you may need additional hardware components for correct presentations in different situations.

This section illustrates a few of the dozens of rigs used by catfish anglers. There are many others. One fun facet of this sport is developing your own rigs. Experiment to improve your presentation using different combinations and configurations of terminal tackle. You may come up with a new rig that will help us all be more successful anglers.

Basic Rigs

When it comes to catfishing rigs, I am, for the most part, a proponent of the K.I.S.S. principle: Keep It Simple, Son! The best catfishing rigs almost always are the simplest. With fewer components, there's less chance that something will fail and cause you to lose a catfish. Simple rigs also are easier to make and easier to cast, plus there's less weight to interfere with natural-looking bait presentations.

Here are tips for putting together some of the most basic rigs.

Egg-Sinker Rig

Application: The egg-sinker rig may be the most commonly used bottom rig for catfishing. By changing the size of the components, you can use it for everything from little bullheads to giant blues and flatheads. With the right size sinker, the bait rests on bottom, and when a cat picks up the bait it feels no tension. This rig works especially well for bottom-fishing in still waters such as ponds and oxbow lakes.

Hardware components: one ½-ounce or larger egg sinker; one size 7 barrel swivel; and one hook of choice.

Rigging: (1) Run your main line through the egg sinker, and tie the line to the barrel swivel. (2) Make a hook leader by tying the hook to an 18- to 36-inch piece of monofilament or fluorocarbon line. The leader line should be somewhat lighter than your main line. (3) Tie the hook leader to the free eye of the barrel swivel.

Details: Use any hook you like with this rig, basing your selection on the type of catfish you're targeting, the bait you're using, and other factors. The size of the egg sinker also can vary. Use a larger sinker where there is heavier current and a smaller one where there is little or no current. Leader length is a matter of personal preference. Longer leaders rise higher above the bottom in current, but tend to snag more. Shorter leaders keep your bait closer to bottom-grubbing cats.

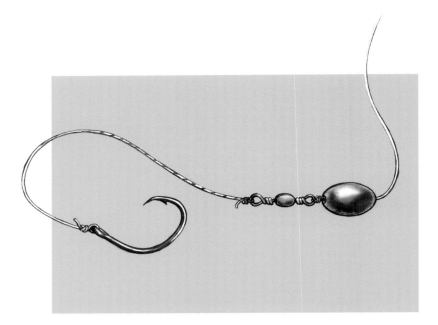

Egg-Sinker Rig

Additional variations are possible. By substituting a bell, or bass-casting, sinker for the egg sinker, you create another rig less likely to roll along the bottom and snag. A walking sinker is useful when fishing waters with current. You can dispense with the swivel and leader line altogether, allowing the sinker to ride snugly against the baited hook if you like. Few anglers use this simplified version, but it works fine in heavy current where a long leader is more likely to get snagged. You also can tie the main line directly to the hook and use a split shot (instead of the swivel) as your sinker stop.

Some anglers also like to place a small plastic bead between the sinker and swivel to create a bit of noise that may attract catfish. The bead also protects the leader knot from abrasion.

Three-Way Rig

Application: The three-way rig is another common bottom presentation. With this rig, your sinker moves along the bottom while your bait rides high. This is a highly versatile presentation, useful for both still-fishing and drift-fishing.

Hardware components: one three-way swivel; one bell, pyramid, bank, or bottom-bouncer sinker; and one hook of choice.

Rigging: (1) Tie your main line to one eye of the three-way swivel. (2) Add leaders of mono or fluorocarbon line—one 12 to 18 inches long and one 24 to 36 inches long—to the other two swivel eyes. (3) Tie the hook to the longer leader line and the sinker to the other.

Details: If a three-way swivel is unavailable, use a barrel swivel instead. Tie the main line to one eye and the two leader lines to the other.

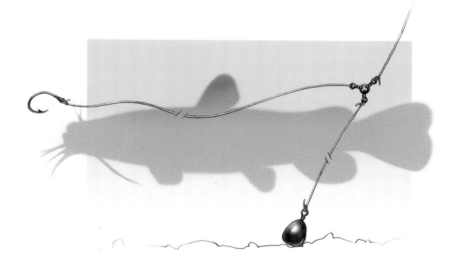

Three-Way Rig

Fixed Float Rig

Fixed Float Rig

Application: Float rigs are great for drifting baits through river cat hideouts or for still-fishing in lakes and ponds. The float suspends the bait at the level you want and serves as a bite indicator.

Hardware components: one peg-on or clip-on float; one hook of choice; and one or two split shot.

Rigging: (1) With a peg-on float, run the line through it first and add the peg to hold the float on the line. (2) Tie the hook to the main line. (3) Crimp the split shot (just enough to sink the bait properly) on the line 3 to 6 inches above the hook. (4) With a clip-on float, clip it on the main line above the split shot at the depth you want to fish.

Details: A fixed float rig is best for fishing water no deeper than your rod is long. You can reel the rig only to the float, which leaves the hook and line dangling below. This makes casting awkward and difficult if the line under the float is too long. The float should be sized to suspend your bait at the level you want. If the bait pulls the float under, use a larger float, but keep the float as small as possible for better bite detection.

Slip Float Rig

Application: A slip, or sliding, float rig is much more versatile than a fixed float rig because it can be cast more easily and fished at much greater depths. Use one anytime the water you are fishing is deeper than the length of your rod.

Hardware components: one bobber stop; one plastic bead; one slip float; one hook of choice; and one or more split shot.

Rigging: (1) Place the bobber stop on the main line. It should be positioned far enough up the line so that the slip float just beneath it will suspend the bait at the desired depth. (2) Run the line through the plastic bead and then through the slip float. (3) Tie the hook at line's end and then crimp on enough split shot a few inches above the hook to hold the float upright in the water and sink the bait.

Details: With this rig, the float slips down to the split shot to allow casting, then slips up to the bobber stop to hold the bait at the correct depth.

A variation of this rig performs well when you're fishing live baitfish for flatheads. Affix the bobber stop, and then run a slip float and an egg sinker up the line. You'll need a big float to hold up this rig. The size of the sinker is determined by the size of the bait. Big baits require bigger sinkers, up to 4 or 5 ounces for a sizeable bluegill or sucker. Tie a barrel swivel beneath the sinker, at the end of the main line. Then, to the bottom eye of the swivel, affix a 10- to 20-inch leader, and to the end of that, a large hook. Impale your baitfish with the hook, just behind the dorsal fin, and you're ready to go after big flatheads.

Slip Float Rig

Advanced Rigs

In certain situations, more complex catfishing rigs provide benefits serious catfish anglers may want to use to their advantage. These include specialty rigs such as the paternoster rig, the big-lake drift rig, and the big-river finesse rig, all of which have applications that make them invaluable for certain types of catfishing.

Paternoster Rig

Application: The paternoster rig, which originated in Europe, is one of the best of all flathead catfish rigs. It's ideal for fishing a large live baitfish such as a bluegill or sucker in shallow water.

Hardware components: one bobber stop and bead; one large slip float such as a Thill 4-inch Big Fish Slider; two size 7 barrel swivels; one 1-ounce bell sinker; and one 8/0 octopus hook.

Rigging: (1) Begin by making a swivel/sinker leader with 17-pound-test mono. Tie one barrel swivel to one end of the line and the bell sinker

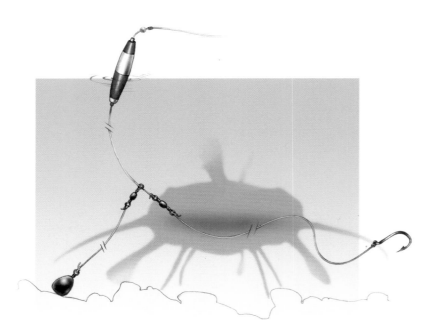

Paternoster Rig

to the other. The finished leader should be about 36 inches long. (2) Make a 20-inch swivel/octopus hook leader in the same manner but using 30-pound-test mono. (3) Place the bobber stop on the main line, followed by the bead and the slip float. (4) Run the main line through the free eye of the swivel on the swivel/sinker leader, and then tie the tag end of the main line to the free eye of the swivel on the swivel/hook leader. The rig is now ready to fish.

Details: The paternoster rig allows the bait to ride higher off the bottom than a simple rig incorporating all hardware components on the main line. The sinker lies on the bottom while the baitfish struggles against the float. Position the bobber stop on the main line in order to leave a foot or two of slack line between the swivel/sinker leader and the float; this gives the bait extra freedom to move about. Use lighter line on the swivel/sinker leader so it will break off if the sinker gets snagged.

Big-Lake Drift Rig

Application: This snagless rig, developed by Texas catfish guide Randle Hall, is excellent for use when drifting for blue catfish on large lakes with little or no current. It is ideal for use in winter when cats are deep and scattered in loose schools.

Hardware components: one 12/0 circle hook; one size 5 stainless-steel split ring; one 2-inch peg-on cigar float; one size 7 barrel swivel; one 1-ounce slinky weight or other flexible snagless sinker; and one size 7 snap swivel. You also need a tube of J-B Weld Liquid Weld Epoxy or a similar product.

Rigging: (1) Attach the split ring to the circle hook eye, and then put two drops of Liquid Weld on each side of the split ring so when it dries, the rings won't pull open. (2) The split ring then is tied to a 36-inch piece of 50-pound-test mono. (3) Put the cigar float on the leader about 10 inches above the hook and ring. The other end of the leader is tied to the barrel swivel. (4) Clip the snap swivel on the slinky weight, run your main line through the eye of this swivel, then tie the main line to the free eye of the barrel swivel. The rig is now ready to fish.

Details: This rig is best used when drifting with the rod in a holder. With the circle hook, the catfish hooks itself. When a fish strikes, leave the rod in the holder, quickly crank the reel handle ten to fifteen times, then pick the rod up and simply start reeling. The fish will be on. Use of the split ring allows the baited hook to swivel, thus allowing better hook penetration. The slinky weight is relatively snagless, making it ideal for drift-fishing, and when the rig moves across the bottom, the cigar float keeps the baited end floating in the strike zone. Hall's favored baits when using this rig are shad cut-bait or triangular "strip baits" made from buffalo, carp, or bonito.

Big-Lake Drift Rig

Big-River Finesse Rig

Application: Mississippi catfish guide Phil King created this superb rig to use when targeting channel and blue catfish holding tight to cover in deep holes of big rivers and river reservoirs. It works well year-round.

Hardware components: one three-way swivel; one size 7 barrel swivel; one 2-ounce bell sinker; and two 5/0 Daiichi Circle-Wide Bleeding Bait hooks.

Rigging: (1) Tie the three-way swivel to your main line. Use 65- to 100-pound-test braided line on your reel for better "feel"; use mono backing next to the spool to prevent slippage. (2) Tie an 8-inch leader of 20-pound-test mono between the bell sinker and one of the free eyes on the three-way swivel. (3) Tie a 12-inch leader of 60-pound-test mono between the remaining three-way swivel eye and the barrel swivel. (4) Tie the two

hooks one above the other and very close together on a 24-inch leader of 60-pound mono, then tie the other end of this leader to the free eye of the barrel swivel. (King snells the two hooks on this leader.) The rig is now ready to fish.

Details: Fishing with this rig is basically a form of finesse fishing, thus the name. Start at the upstream end of a river hole and drift through after lowering the rig to the bottom. Most cats hold beside river-bottom timber

Big-River Finesse Rig

and rocks, which "telegraph" signals through the braided line to the angler above. The angler must be attentive at all times, raising or lowering the rig with the rod tip so he maintains feel with the rig below and keeps it bouncing across the pieces of cover and structure without hanging. King uses two baits with this rig: either a big bloody chunk of fresh chicken liver or a "catfish sandwich." The latter is simply the innards of a big skipjack herring sandwiched between two side fillets from the same baitfish.

CHAPTER SEVEN

Boats

Species-specific boats have been around a long time. Boat manufacturers have cultivated larger market shares by producing crafts with layouts and features geared to help catch more of a particular fish more comfortably. Many specialty boats are available for bass anglers, walleye fishermen, striper fanatics, and even panfishermen. But even with 7.5 million anglers who regard themselves as catfish fans, the boating industry has largely ignored this vast species-specific market. For that reason, serious catmen have traditionally had to take whatever boat was available, reshape it, and make it work.

Fortunately, change is in the wind. Catfish anglers finally are receiving some attention they deserve from the powers that be in the fishing industry, and a wide variety of catfish-specific goods now are available, including boats made specifically with catfishermen in mind.

One such boat I've had an opportunity to use is the aluminum V-Cat by SeaArk Boats of Monticello, Arkansas, one of the first companies to come out with a species-specific catfish craft. This V-hull boat, rated for a 150-horsepower outboard, has many design features that make it an excellent cat boat:

- **60-gallon aerated livewell.** A necessity when tournament fishing or keeping small cats for the dinner table.
- **Baitwell.** The V-Cat's 12-gallon aerated baitwell provides adequate space for keeping a few dozen baitfish lively, a must on any cat boat.
- **Heavy-duty, all-welded construction.** Provides durability on big rivers and other rough, rocky and/or timber-laden waters often frequented by catfish anglers.
- **Large size.** The 20-foot, 1-inch length, 94-inch beam, and 72-inch bottom width provide lots of room for two or more anglers and all their gear. Weight capacity is an ample 2,000 pounds.
- **Fold-down pedestal seats and rear bench seat.** Provide comfort during a long day or night on the water.
- **Navigation lights.** Must-have when night fishing for cats.
- **Anchor locker, two aft storage boxes, and bow deck storage.** Cubbyholes for stashing essentials out of the way when running and trailering.
- **No carpeting.** Carpet might seem like a nice feature, but you won't want it in a cat boat that's constantly soiled with blood, fish slime, and oily cut-bait.

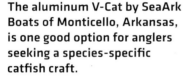

The aluminum V-Cat by SeaArk Boats of Monticello, Arkansas, is one good option for anglers seeking a species-specific catfish craft.

While SeaArk's V-Cat and other boats like it certainly are a step in the right direction, there are many additional features that could be added to create a boat even more in tune with the catfish angler's needs. For example:

- **Bait cooler.** A place to keep cut-bait fresh. Should have a drain and drop-in grate. Put ice on the bottom, add the grate, and keep baitfish pieces on the grate so they don't get soggy.
- **Bait preparation station.** Also for cut-bait fishing. Put it close to the cooler and baitwell, please, and include a cutting board.
- **Washdown system.** When slime, bait, and blood get the boat messy, pump in fresh water to hose down the floor and decks. This is standard on saltwater boats and should be on cat boats.
- **Rod holders.** Solidly mounted, durable, stainless holders at strategic points around the boat to hold rods when drifting and still-fishing.
- **Non-skid floor and deck.** One fat cat can slime a boat and make moving around feel like walking on banana peels. A sand-impregnated gel coat or another nonskid surface would help.

The V-Cat's baitwell provides a handy place for keeping several dozen baitfish.

CAT BOAT OPTIONS

Catfish anglers use boats of all shapes and sizes. Here are some of the many options available.

- **Johnboats.** These flat, stable craft, typically aluminum, are perhaps the most commonly used type of catfish boat. They're easily customized for catfishing, and varied sizes allow use anywhere from farm ponds to big rivers.

- **Pontoon boats or party barges.** Great on big open lakes where water sometimes get rough and whenever extra space is needed for several anglers to fish together. Also good when youngsters are along, thanks to wide, stable decks and side rails.

- **Canoes.** When fishing small streams or backcountry waters with poor or no access facilities, a lightweight canoe is ideal.

- **Center console boats.** These open fishing boats are built to take on rough offshore waters while pursuing ocean fish, making them great for big-river and big-lake catfishing as well. Rod holders, downriggers, and other gear are common fittings onboard.

- **Bass boats.** Made with low, sleek profiles and built to fish with two or three anglers on board, bass boats can be used in many catfishing situations.

- **Fish and ski.** This family fishing and recreational boat has enough power to pull a skier or two and to get to your catfishing spot in short order.

- **Dinghy.** Usually small (less than 10 feet), dinghies are easy to carry on a car top or store on board a cruiser. They're great when targeting white cats and blues in marshes and coastal rivers.

- **Sound insulation.** Catfish are much more sensitive to sounds and vibration than other sportfish. Without carpeting (which we don't want), sound insulation is lost. Adding some insulation between the hull and floor would help. Also, storage-box lids need valves so they don't slam shut.

- **Bigger livewell.** Cat anglers who fish tournaments need something capable of holding a wide-headed fish that may weigh 50 pounds or more, maybe several such fish. A big rectangular box with a big opening would be great.

- **Bigger, round baitwell.** Doesn't have to be huge—20 gallons would suffice—but it should be rounded to keep shad and other delicate baitfish from "rednosing" in the corners. A gentle, bubbling aerator would be best.

- **Fold-down top.** An inexpensive Bimini top would sure be nice on rainy or sunny days.

- **Standard electronics.** Every cat man needs them—a graph, surface temperature gauge, and GPS, minimum.

- **Blacklights.** To illuminate fluorescent mono when night fishing for easier bite detection.

Sounds like what we need is a big saltwater fishing boat, right? That certainly is an option, but in the not-too-distant future, chances are we'll be seeing more boats specially made for catfishing that include a variety of the features mentioned above. In the meantime, check out SeaArk's cat boats and those now manufactured by other companies. Many have features that can make your catfishing excursions more enjoyable and successful.

Opposite: Pontoon boats are among the many specialty crafts used by catfish anglers.

CHAPTER EIGHT

Bait Guide

Catfish anglers use an incredible number of baits to entice their quarry. Natural baits such as fish and worms sometimes adorn their hooks, but just as often, the bait may be something that seems totally weird, such as a piece of hot dog, a chunk of soap, or a smelly home brew of blood, guts, and cheese. Catfish like them all.

Natural Baits

When fishing for catfish using natural baits, remember the bait equation: fresh bait + proper presentation = more cats. Without fresh bait, either live or freshly killed, you'll find it difficult to catch catfish consistently.

Try to determine natural foods favored by catfish in the bodies of water you fish. Fisheries biologists, bait-shop owners, and anglers can help in this regard, so seek their advice. Ask what the fish eat and when. A flathead lake may have lots of bluegills but few shad, so bluegills are more likely to yield a catch. If freezing temperatures cause a die-off, blue cats and channels may gorge on shad, making that the best choice.

You also should match the type of bait to the type of catfish you hope to catch. For example, if catching a trophy-class flathead is your goal, using catalpa worms for an enticement isn't wise. Small flatheads love them, but they aren't on the big flathead's menu. Live fish baits are the key to success in this case. If you want some channel cats for a fish fry, your bait selection can run the gamut from stinkbaits to night crawlers. But if you have your eye on a heavyweight river blue, you'd be smarter to use shad or skipjack herring.

Some good baits are available from bait dealers or fish farms. Using these allows you to spend more time fishing, less time finding bait. If the bait you need can't be purchased, however, you'll have to learn ways to obtain your own and allot some time for bait-catching before fishing.

If shad rank high on the local bait list, invest in a good cast net, and learn to use it properly. Some excellent baits—skipjacks, sunfish, and bullheads, for example—can be caught on small lures or baited hooks. Special traps may be required to catch crayfish, creek chubs, and other favored baits, but some bait animals, such as frogs, can be caught by hand. Check local regulations to determine what's legal, and then learn the best methods to catch what you need.

Most anglers try to catch what they need in advance of their fishing trip, and do what's necessary to keep it lively or fresh. This may be as simple as icing down skipjacks in a cooler or keeping frogs in a wet burlap bag, or as elaborate as constructing special aerated tanks for housing live baitfish. If the bait of preference is unobtainable, a substitute can be found before the trip is made.

Fresh-caught natural baits such as this goldeye will attract catfish much quicker than old or frozen baits.

Frozen baits rarely work as well as fresh-caught baits, but when bait such as herring is plentiful, consider freezing some for times of need. Vacuum-packaging units such as the Tilia FoodSaver can maintain surplus baits in near-fresh condition for months, and are well worth the meager investment.

The bottom line is this: Use the freshest bait possible to improve your odds for success. Try to catch some bait onsite before you start fishing, for this is the freshest of all. But be prepared in case your efforts fail.

Skipjack herring

Bullhead

Longear sunfish

Following are details about some excellent natural baits for putting catfish in your boat.

Live Fish

Live fish top the list of the most enticing catfish baits, and with good reason. A catfish 24 inches or longer, regardless of species, sustains itself on a diet comprised almost exclusively of other fish. There simply are no better baits for trophy cats.

Shad and herring. Throughout much of their range, large blue cats feed almost exclusively on shad, herring, and other schooling baitfish. Channel cats and flatheads relish them too.

Catch these baitfish using a cast net, tiny jigs and spoons, or a sabiki rig (see sidebar on page 81). To remain healthy, they must be kept uncrowded in highly oxygenated water. Use a large, round, well-insulated, aerated tank with cool stream or lake water, or rig a perforated garbage can to carry them alongside your boat. A gallon of water supports about four large baitfish.

Bullheads. Bullheads are the main prey of flatheads in many waters where both are common, and many catfish anglers are aware of this. Bullheads have been used as flathead bait for more than one hundred years, and they sometimes attract big blues and channel cats as well. They're tough, easy to keep alive in a bait tank, and are readily caught on hook and line using chicken liver or worms.

Sunfish. Live sunfish are hot catfish baits on many waters, especially for large flatheads. One of the most widely used species is the ubiquitous green sunfish, sometimes called a ricefield slick or shade perch, which is extremely abundant, hardy, and easy to catch on hook and line or by seining. Other species used as cat bait where law permits include bluegills, redears, pumpkinseeds, longear sunfish, and spotted sunfish.

Suckers and chubs. Suckers or creek chubs, 6 to 12 inches long, also make great catfish bait because they're active, hardy, and a favored food of large cats, especially big flatheads and channels. In some parts of the country, both are often available at bait shops. They also can be seined from creeks or small rivers or caught on tiny hooks baited with bits of worm.

Other fish. Among "bait-store" baits, goldfish, fathead minnows, and large shiners are hard to beat. The rosy red, or pink, minnow—a special orange-colored variety of the fathead minnow—is a special favorite of many anglers, and the Black Salty baitfish—a specially raised goldfish tolerant of saltwater—is quickly becoming popular for both fresh and brackish water. Other good cat baits include small carp, mooneyes, goldeyes, alewives, ciscoes, killifish, American eels, madtoms, and stonecats.

Live fish tip: The attractiveness of live-fish baits can be improved by snipping the spiny fins off, causing the baitfish to bleed and flounder in the water. As the blood trail flows, catfish are attracted.

Creek chub

Rosy-red, or pink, minnows

Cut-Baits

Pieces sliced from freshly killed baitfish are excellent enticements for catfish, especially blues and channels. Catfish anglers call these cut-baits. When a chunk or fillet is placed in the water, body fluids seep out that catfish can smell and taste from long distances. Oily fish—shad, herring, suckers, etc.—make the best cut-baits, but when these aren't available, almost any baitfish will work.

Cut-bait is prepared many ways. Some anglers fillet strips from a baitfish's sides or belly. Others cut the bait in chunks. Still others use only the entrails, or "gizzards." Vary what you use until you determine what

Cut-bait can be prepared in chunks, fillets, or other ways, all of which will catch catfish.

Night crawlers

catfish want. If fillets don't work, try using heads or tails. If these don't work, try other pieces.

Match the bait's size to the catfish. In waters with few cats over 5 pounds, use small chunks or strips of cut-bait. Where bigger cats are common, 4- to 6-inch baits aren't out of place.

When using fillets for bait, leave the skin on, and then thread the fillet on the hook. For chunks, slice crosswise through the fish, dividing it into head, midsection, and tail pieces, or just head and tail. Hook the head through the eyes or mouth. When using tail or body pieces, run the hook completely through, leaving the point exposed.

Cut-bait tip: One great cat-catching rig for many situations is just a lead jig head with a piece of cut-bait on the hook. Cast and retrieve with a lift-hop presentation for active cats, or work it vertically beneath a boat when the bite is slow.

Earthworms

Night crawlers and other earthworms are irresistible to channel cats, small flatheads, small blues, and bullheads. They also can be fished on special rigs to catch trophy-class flatheads. Buy them in bait shops or gather your own in damp places using a shovel or rake. Store in insulated containers in a refrigerator, ice chest, or other cool place.

Worm tip: Use a hypodermic syringe or specially made worm blower to inflate a worm and make it a more effective bait. Adding a shot of air to the tail lifts the worm up so it's more visible to catfish. You can lift the whole crawler above bottom by adding a second shot of air under the collar. Your sinker stays on bottom while your bait rides high.

Crayfish

Crayfish are hard-to-beat catfish baits. In many lakes, ponds, and streams, they comprise an important dietary component for all major catfish species. Collect them by turning rocks on a stream bottom and grabbing them with your hands, a dip net, or a seine. Crayfish traps baited with fish parts in a cheesecloth bag also work. Keep crayfish lively in a minnow bucket with wet leaves or moss in the bottom.

Crayfish

Crayfish tip: Break off the pincers of crayfish to keep them from grabbing objects on the bottom. For small cats, try using a broken-off tail or piece of peeled tail instead of the whole crayfish.

Frogs

Few baits are more effective for trophy channel cats than live frogs. Any aquatic species can be used, including bullfrogs, green frogs, pickerel frogs, and leopard, or grass, frogs. But check local regulations before collecting as most states have seasons and limits.

If your bait shop doesn't carry frogs (some do), catch them by driving a rural road on a warm, rainy, spring night. Pick an area where traffic volume is low, and take a friend along. When you spot the quarry, the passenger hops out, catches it, and places it in a dampened burlap bag or pillow case. It's possible to gather dozens of frogs this way on a single night.

Bullfrog

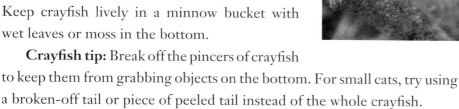

You also can catch frogs by hand or with a small-mesh dip net along shores of ponds, lakes, backwaters, bayous, and streams. Store them in a cool place to keep them lively.

Hook frogs through a foreleg, hind leg, or the lips. If a sinker is added, it should be small enough that it won't inhibit the frog's natural action.

Frog tip: A live frog struggling at the surface is a morsel few catfish can resist. If the bait swims for bottom, use your rod to lift it so it will continue swimming topside. Smashing surface strikes result.

Catalpa worm

Leech

Catalpa Worms

The catalpa worm is the caterpillar of the catalpa sphinx moth. In spring, female moths lay eggs on the undersides of catalpa leaves. In ten to fourteen days, each egg hatches into a tiny caterpillar with a whale of an appetite for catalpa leaves. The velvety larvae grow quickly to 3 inches or so. Catfish anglers begin gathering them in April, May, or June, depending on latitude. Most non-anglers are eager to get rid of them, but ask permission before collecting on private property. A second hatch of catalpa worms often takes place in autumn.

Gathering catalpa worms is simple. Those on low branches can be picked from the leaves. For those higher up, use a long cane pole to slap the leaves. This produces a shower of falling worms. When they're grounded, gather them and store in a cool container with a few catalpa leaves.

Catalpa worm tip: Although live catalpa worms are only available a few months each year, they can be stored for off-season use. Catfish relish them live or dead. After collecting the worms, drop them in a container of ice water to retain their color. Then put twenty to twenty-five of them in a quart zip-seal bag and fill the bag with corn meal. Place the bag in the freezer, and pull it out again when you're ready to fish.

Leeches

Large leeches, 5 to 10 inches long, are excellent cat baits. They are exceptionally tough and stay on hooks very well. In north-central states, leeches are readily available from bait dealers, but in other areas you'll probably have to collect your own. Ponds with lush growths of cattails and lily pads are good places to find them.

Store leeches in cool water in a minnow bucket or Styrofoam cooler. Check them daily and discard any that are dead. The best bait leeches squirm actively when held.

Leech tip: To catch leeches, put fresh beef liver in a burlap sack and toss it into shallow water. Leeches will squirm through the fabric to reach the bait.

SABIKI RIG FISHING TIPS

Sabiki rigs, sometimes called piscator rigs, are great tools for catching shad, herring, and other baitfish. These are pre-tied rigs with a main line to which several dropper lines are attached. At the end of each dropper line is a small lure with a tiny hook and a body made of feathers or plastic. A swivel at the main line's end provides a place to tie a sinker so the rig can be dropped quickly to the bottom. If you place the rig near shad or skipjacks, they're quick to strike the tiny lures, and it's not unusual to bring up three or four baitfish at once.

Many companies make sabiki rigs, but the rig I use most is the Daiichi Bleeding Bait Sabiki Rig, which has red hooks. I asked T. J. Stallings at Daiichi to provide tips for fishing these rigs, and he offered several you'll find useful.

"Using the right tackle can really make a difference," Stallings says. "A 6-foot, 6-inch or 7-foot, medium-action spinning rod makes handling the rig easier, and the softer tip keeps light pressure on head-shaking bait. Use light line, too, which sinks faster. Sixteen-pound-test is plenty for most bait."

Stallings notes that better-quality sabiki rigs feature "one pull" packaging.

"To use one, start by adding a slip bead like the Tru-Turn Soft Feel Glow Bead on your line. This will prevent winding the rig up into the rod guides. Choose any color bead but red, which will attract the bait away from the rig.

"Next, open the package, and tie the rig onto a swivel. Pull the rig out slowly until all of it is out of the package. The bottom of the sabiki rig will have a small snap that will connect to your sinker."

There is no need to set the hook(s) when fishing a sabiki rig. "The tiny hooks will do their job quickly," says Stallings. "Just lower the rig and retrieve slowly after you feel several bites. Trimming the tails of the lures about $1/16$ inch sometimes increases hook-ups."

If you're fishing for bait near banks, you may have to cast the rigs around structure where shad and other baitfish hide. Use extreme caution when you do so, and warn fellow anglers in the boat. "Swing" or underhand cast the rig toward your target.

"Overhand casting a rig with six tiny hooks is a quick way to pierce some ears," Stallings laughs.

When you've finished catching bait, remove the sinker from the rig and clip the snap to your hook holder on the rod or around the foot of your reel. Now connect the hooks to each other, and reel the rig up until snug. Be careful not to put a bend in your rod.

A wide variety of good catfish baits are readily available in grocery stores.

Grocery Store Baits

Obtaining natural baits can be difficult at times. Shad may be plentiful one day but gone the next. Herring may have migrated to parts unknown. Sunfish may refuse to bite. The bait shop may be out of worms or minnows.

Fortunately, some good baits are available at the supermarket. I call them grocery store baits, and though they don't attract the attention of heavyweight blues, flatheads, and channel cats as often as fresh fish baits, they do so often enough that you should consider using them whenever the need arises.

I learned about these baits from fellow catfishing enthusiasts, each of whom shared some tips to help you get the most from these readily available cat-catchers.

Hot Dogs

"Did you know cats would eat dogs?"

Joe Drose asked me that while I was fighting a nice blue cat on South Carolina's Lake Moultrie, one of the famous Santee-Cooper lakes. Drose has been guiding catfishermen on these waters since Methuselah was a baby. He had baited our hooks with chunks of hot dogs, which seemed to me rather unusual for a man noted as a trophy-cat expert.

"Won't we just catch little cats using hot dogs for bait?" I asked.

"We may catch some small fish," Drose replied, "but there's an equally good chance we'll nail a trophy, too. Big blue catfish often feed on small mussels, and though a piece of herring the same size as one of these clams may work better, a clam-size chunk of hot dog often works, too. I've caught catfish up to 70 pounds using hot dogs for bait. And believe it or not, the cheaper brands of hot dogs—those made with turkey or chicken—work best. They don't seem to like all-beef."

How to fish: Drose uses an egg-sinker rig made with a sturdy 3/0 to 5/0 Kahle hook when fishing hot dog baits. He casts this to a likely spot and allows it to sit up to fifteen minutes. If no bite is forthcoming, Drose moves to another spot and tries again.

Chicken Liver

Corinth, Mississippi, catfish guide Phil King has targeted big cats in the Tennessee River system for decades. He fishes a variety of baits, including dip baits, shad, and skipjack herring. At least one grocery store bait—fresh chicken liver—also figures into his angling.

"I start using fresh chicken livers around the first of May and continue to use them through late fall," he said. "The blood in fresh liver attracts catfish from a long distance, and it's not unusual to take big blue or channel catfish when still-fishing in a good area or slow-drifting through deep holes or along ledges."

How to fish: King's terminal tackle typically consists of a double-hook rig, with one bait placed several feet above another on the main leader.

A treble hook attached to your line with a swivel is another good rig. Unsnap the swivel, remove the hook, push the eye of the hook through the liver so the liver is impaled on the three barbs, and then reattach the hook to the swivel. Add a sinker above the hook to carry the bait to the bottom and you're ready for action.

Chicken livers are among the most popular and effective of all store-bought baits.

Bacon

Roger Aziz Jr. of Methuen, Massachusetts, is one of the best tidewater catfish anglers in the country. White catfish are the most common species in these brackish waters, and Aziz has caught several that qualified as line-class records. Some were caught using bacon for bait.

"Bacon works best in spring," he says, "because there aren't any herring or shad moving in the rivers. I like to use a very sharp Kahle hook and get as much bacon on it as I can. A sharp hook will cut through the bacon and give you a good hookset. And I've found that hickory-smoked bacon works best."

How to fish: "My favorite rig uses a 2- to 3-ounce bass-casting sinker,

SOAP FOR BAIT?

When Procter & Gamble introduced Ivory Soap in 1879, the folks at the company probably never imagined their product would become a popular catfish bait. But that's what happened, and for more than a century, bars of this "99.44% pure" hand cleaner have been a staple in the bait boxes of hardcore cat men.

Although Ivory is the brand most often used, Octagon and Zote soaps also work great. These also are "pure" soaps without additives. Some catfishermen I know use old-fashioned lye soap made at home, and it, too, seldom fails to coax a bite from hungry cats.

How to fish: Old-timers on the rivers I fished as a youngster often baited trotlines with chunks cut from bars of Ivory soap. My uncle was one of these old-timers, and when we ran lines he'd baited in this fashion, it wasn't unusual to find a cat on every other hook, including some huge specimens. A small piece threaded on a hook works equally well for rod-and-reel anglers.

Ivory Soap really does catch catfish!

or a no-roll sinker that I mold myself with a swivel in the top," Aziz says. "A black rubber bead is placed between the sinker and a 3/0 Kahle hook. I fish this right on the bottom, letting the weight ride right against the hook. The sinker lays flat on the bottom, and the bait rides a few inches above it."

Squid

In winter, when live baits are hard to come by, anglers must rely more on various grocery store baits. Randle Hall, a Texas catfish guide, told me, "I started experimenting and found that squid really works. I use non-cleaned squid bought at the supermarket, half a squid per hook."

How to fish: Hall fishes this unusual but effective bait on the big-lake drift rig.

More Grocery Store Baits

I've never tried it, but you might want to give Hormel Spam a go sometime. On August 3, 2001, Charles Ashley Jr. of Marion, Arkansas, used a chunk of this spicy canned meat to catch a 116-pound, 12-ounce, world-record blue cat in the Mississippi River.

"My father used Spam for catfish bait, and so did my grandfather," said Ashley. "I rarely use anything else."

Other grocery store baits proven to catch cats include fresh and frozen shrimp; smelly cheeses such as Limburger and sharp cheddar; golden raisins and green grapes, both of which are superb, if unusual, summer cat baits; and even bubble gum (Bazooka and Bubble Yum rate high in some areas).

The fact is, you'll probably hook a big catfish sooner or later no matter what bait you dangle in the water. So next time you're at the grocery, pick up something new and experiment. If the fish don't bite, you can snack on the bait!

Doughs, Dips, and Other Stinkbaits

Every dedicated catfish angler has a favorite stinkbait he swears will outperform all others. Secret recipes for proven potions are passed down from generation to generation with explicit instructions never to reveal the ingredients.

Stinkbaits also are produced by a number of manufacturers. There are scores available in different forms—dip baits, doughbaits, chunk baits, and more.

Small channel cats and blue cats are most likely to be caught when fishing stinkbaits. These young fish eat a wider variety of foods than heavyweight adults. As channel and blue cats grow, their diet becomes less varied, consisting mostly of live baitfish and other abundant forage. Flatheads rarely scavenge, so stinkbaits rarely catch them.

The method used for fishing stinkbait is determined primarily by the bait's consistency.

Doughbaits

Doughbaits have bread-dough consistency. Many don't stay on the hook well when casting, especially during hot weather. Cloth doughbait bags and spring-wound bait-holder treble hooks are helpful, but it's best to use only thick doughbait mixtures that can be molded around a regular hook to form a firm ball that won't fly off.

To properly fish doughbaits, move the bait very little. Give careful thought to finding prime catfishing areas, then after you cast, allow the bait to sit fifteen to twenty minutes. Doughbaits must melt to lay a scent trail. If there are no bites in the specified time, relocate.

Stinkbaits are available in many commercial forms, but creating homemade mixes is a favorite hobby of many cat men.

Home recipe: Make your own doughbait using refrigerated bread dough or by mixing flour and water to form a thick dough. Add flavoring catfish like—anise oil, commercial catfish scents, blood, rancid cheese, etc.—then roll the dough into balls and store in a loosely sealed plastic container.

Dip Baits

Dip baits have the consistency of, well, dip—the kind you dunk potato chips in. Because they won't cling to a hook, they're fished using special lures called "catfish worms." These are plastic grubs with rings, dimples, or holes that hold the dip bait. A hook in the grub's tail holds the catfish.

The best worms, such as Cat Tracker Bait Company's Tubie 2000, can be rigged using a treble hook or single hook, an important trait for anglers who practice catch-and-release catting. Catfish worms come in many colors, and some are impregnated with attractive flavorings such as anise or shrimp.

Most catfish worms come prerigged or have hooks and worms together in the package. Follow package directions for rigging, and then tie an 18- to 24-inch monofilament leader (30- to 40-pound-test) to the hook. Run your main line through an egg sinker (½ to 4 ounces, depending on current), then tie a barrel or snap swivel to the line's end. When fishing with trebles, the snap allows you to quickly replace a rig swallowed by a catfish.

Tie the worm leader to the swivel and you're ready to fish. Stir the bait with a stick until smooth, then dry the worm and dip it in the bait. (Drying the lure helps the bait stick better.) Push it around with the stick until thoroughly coated, forcing bait into all the worm's pores or grooves. Cast the lure, let it sink to the bottom, and then wait for a catfish to home in on the scent. Dip baits melt quickly, so dry and dunk your lure frequently to keep it covered.

Home recipe: One productive dip bait is a mixture of chicken liver and Limburger or some other smelly cheese. Combine equal measures in a plastic container, mash together, cover, poke some holes in the lid, and then place in a warm location for several days. Don't get this bait on you, though, as the smell can't be scrubbed off.

Sponge Baits

Sponge baits are thinner than dip baits. A sponged-covered treble hook is used to soak up the bait for fishing. Catfish scent formulas also can be fished in this manner.

Fishing sponge baits is simple. Impale a 1-inch square piece of sponge on a hook, dip it in the bait, mash the sponge with a stick till it's saturated, and then cast the sponge rig to your fishing spot. The bait bleeds out more slowly than a typical dip bait, but quicker than a good doughbait, so check your sponge every ten minutes or so to be sure it's well soaked with bait.

Home recipe: Instead of throwing dead minnows away after a day's fishing, keep them in a jar and allow them to decompose until only an oily residue remains. This makes great sponge bait. The oil from a can of sardines or tuna also works.

Chunk Baits

Chunk baits are solid grape-size baits. They generally melt slowly, so a cat must be close to find your offering unless you have time to wait. This fact, however, makes chunk baits highly desirable for baiting trotlines, limblines, and other set lines.

Home recipe: Make your own chunk baits by slicing inexpensive hot dogs into 1-inch pieces and putting them in a jar. Add two packages of strawberry Kool-Aid (unsweetened) and several cloves of garlic. Fill the jar with water, and allow the wieners to marinate overnight.

Tube Baits

Tube baits are commercially manufactured products packaged in long, soft-plastic tubes like toothpaste. They're usually fished in specially made hollow lures that come in a variety of shapes and sizes for different fishing situations. Narrow slits or holes permit bait to be squeezed

BLOOD BAITS

Blood in the water attracts catfish just like it attracts sharks. Thus, blood baits have long been used by ardent catfish anglers, especially for tempting small channel cats, blue cats, and bullheads. (Flatheads prefer live food and rarely are caught on blood baits.)

Beef, turkey, and chicken blood are commonly used and can be obtained at little cost from butchers or meat-processing plants.

To turn the blood into bait, pour half an inch in a shallow pan, then refrigerate until the blood coagulates. The thickened blood then is cut into strips or chunks and stored in a plastic container. When needed, a piece is pinched off and threaded on a hook. Blood keeps indefinitely when frozen. Bait can be thawed and refrozen each trip until it's gone. Blood baits also are available commercially from several manufacturers.

Blood bait's main advantage is the fact that it attracts catfish quickly over long distances. Its most serious drawback is the fact that it just won't stay on your hook. To overcome this problem, wrap light string around the hooked bait or enclose the bait in a small square of nylon stocking. Without the string or nylon cover, casting blood bait is virtually impossible, and even slight currents force constant rebaiting. Blood bait is also extremely messy, and you need a towel handy to keep clean when baiting hooks.

Fortunately, blood bait's disadvantages are largely outweighed by its great cat appeal. For finicky cats in quiet water, few baits work better.

in, and small holes let the bait melt slowly into the water. Tube baits also can be applied to sponge hooks, catfish worms, or even into mouths and gills of minnows and shad.

Tube baits offer several advantages over other stinkbaits. For catters who abhor the waiting game, tube bait lures can be repeatedly cast and retrieved just like other artificials, but work them very slowly. Lure fishing works exceptionally well in heavy currents and hot weather where other stinkbaits fail.

CHAPTER NINE

Seasonal Patterns

To target catfish successfully, especially trophy-size cats, anglers must acquire an in-depth understanding of the primary feeding patterns specific to each species during each season. What are catfish likely to be eating? When? Where? Armed with the answers to these questions, an angler can have reasonable expectations of finding and hooking catfish. Without these answers, luck alone determines the outcome.

Channel Catfish

Frogs for Big Spring Cats

In spring, frogs gather by the thousands to breed in shallow, weedy waters. Some types, like the leopard frog, breed early in the season, while others such as the bullfrog don't start reproductive activities until spring is farther along. For this reason, frogs are available in huge numbers for two to three months, and whenever and wherever they are singing, you can be sure channel cats are nearby. These whiskerfish prowl the shallows day and

A lively frog hooked through a foreleg is one of the best baits for big channel cats.

night, gorging on frogs. And because they're hugging edge areas, even the biggest cats are easy to find and catch on frog baits.

Most states restrict the harvest of frogs in various ways, so check the regulations in your area before catching bait. Leopard frogs, often called grass frogs, are favorites for catfish bait in many areas, but any aquatic species will work. The best are larger ones such as bullfrogs, leopard frogs, green frogs, and pickerel frogs. If possible, select those 4 to 6 inches long, an ideal size for jumbo channel cats.

Frogs can be hooked through both lips or in the thigh, but hooking the amphibian through a foreleg maintains maximum swimming ability, making the frog a more enticing bait. I prefer a 5/0 to 6/0 weedless hook with wire guard to prevent snagging in weeds or brush, but a similar-size Kahle hook works as well. Add one or two split shot on the line 12 inches above the hook to complete the rig. No bobber is necessary.

Fish shallow ponds stocked with channel cats to make the most of this pattern. Rig the frog and cast it near shoreline cover using a spinning or baitcasting outfit. The frog will swim for the bottom, where it's easily spotted by foraging cats. If you don't get a bite within a few minutes, raise your rod tip to stir the frog into action again. Most strikes come quickly when the bait is swimming.

Hoppers on Top in Summer

If channel cats can find concentrations of favored foods on the surface, they'll feed on top. If you don't believe it, drop by a catfish aquaculture operation at feeding time. Fish farmers fatten cats on a diet of floating chow, and when they scatter the food over a pond, you'll see thousands of whiskers as cats rise to feed.

One natural food that encourages a topwater bite is grasshoppers. When something spooks them from their grassy haunts, they'll leap, fly, and often dive right in the water. If one lands in water inhabited by channel cats, it won't sit long before a cat comes up to eat it. Catfish sometimes feed on other insects as well—mayflies, moths, caddis larvae, hellgrammites, and more. But these puny bugs don't appeal to larger cats the way a fat hopper does.

Catfish sometimes turn their noses up at small insects, but big grasshoppers are quickly eaten.

Grasshoppers usually live in tall grass and are relatively easy to catch. A good trick an uncle taught me is to spread an old flannel blanket across the grass and then drive the hoppers to it. Their feet stick in the fabric. A fine-mesh insect net works, too. Keep the grasshoppers in a cricket cage until you're ready to use them.

As catfish baits, grasshoppers work equally on the surface, at mid-depths, or on the bottom. But fishing them as topwater baits is the ultimate thrill. You watch the wake of a catfish homing in on your bait. You see the fish boil beneath it. You witness the hookset. Catfishing doesn't get better than that.

To fish a grasshopper this way, secure it to a 2/0 or 3/0 Aberdeen hook with a small rubber band (the type used in little girls' pigtails or by people who wear braces). Then flip the insect beside shallow cover using a fly rod or spinning outfit. No weight, bobber, or other terminal tackle is necessary unless you need something to help you make longer casts. As soon as the bug hits the water, prepare for the strike. Cats hit hoppers hard and fast, like a largemouth blasting a topwater plug. Within seconds of each cast, you'll be enjoying a rod-bending battle, and watching the action as it happens makes it all unforgettable.

River Baits for Autumn's Eaters

Finding autumn channel cats in lakes sometimes proves baffling. The fish may be deep one day, shallow the next, especially in bodies of water that experience fall turnover. The turnover phenomenon is absent in small mountain rivers, however, a fact that makes these waters great places to fish in fall. You won't find trophy-size channels too often, but if you want a mess

Some of the best baits for autumn catfish in rivers are crayfish and other forage animals that live in the river.

of small cats for a fish fry, give these streams a try. Channel cats to 5 pounds are super-abundant in many clear, cool upland rivers.

The best baits for mountain river catfishing are found in the river you're fishing. In some areas, crayfish are abundant and easy to collect by turning over rocks. You may find hellgrammites under rocks, too. These black, centipede-like larvae of the dobsonfly are relished by channel cats. Pick them from the rocks, being careful to avoid the pincers, and store them, like crayfish, in a minnow bucket or other container with damp leaves or moss in the bottom. Hellgrammites are tough and stay on the hook well. You often can catch several catfish on one bait.

Creek chubs and suckers thrive in clear, cool streams as well, and both are favored foods of fall channel cats. Sometimes you can catch them on tiny hooks baited with a bit of worm, but if it's legal where you fish, a seine or minnow trap works better.

Most mountain stream channel cats hold in scour holes just downstream from shallow riffles.

Cats sometimes feed in riffles and pools but seldom stay long. Holes, on the other hand, provide depth, current, food, and security. The hole's deepest portion is the den or bedroom area, where cats rest out of the current. The upper end is the kitchen or dining room where cats usually feed.

Rocks, logs, and other cover in a hole's deeper, upstream end are especially attractive to actively feeding fish. Cats ambush prey from behind these current breaks. Cover objects where current is lighter or water is shallower aren't as likely to hold active catfish.

Wading and casting to fish-holding structure and cover is a great way to fish these holes, and in most situations, a bobber/drift presentation works well. When fishing with crayfish, hook the bait through the tail for a natural backward retrieve. Hook hellgrammites under the collar. Chubs and suckers can be hooked through the lips or behind the dorsal fin. No matter what bait you use, leave the hook point exposed for better hookups.

Position the bobber so the bait hangs just above the bottom. Add enough weight to hold the bait down, and then drift the rig alongside cover and structure. With practice, you'll become adept at steering the bait past holding areas without worrying about hang-ups.

Winter's Coldkill Shad

Gizzard and threadfin shad, both favored channel cat foods, are poorly suited for life in cold water. If the temperature dips below 45 degrees F in waters where they live, shad become cold-stressed. If the water temperature continues dropping, thousands of shad die. This phenomenon, a yearly event on many lakes and rivers, is known as "coldkill" or "winterkill."

Channel cat feeding activity drops markedly when the water temperature drops below 48 degrees, but when coldkill starts, they throw off their lethargy and flock to shad schools like bears around a salmon run. Dying baitfish are quickly gobbled down by waiting cats. The pattern may last a day or a month, depending on the weather. But while it lasts, fishing for big channel cats is excellent.

The first order of business for coldkill anglers is obtaining shad for bait. A cast net sometimes is used for this purpose, but often this isn't necessary; the dead and dying baitfish can be scooped up in a dip net. Use only those that are relatively fresh, and keep them on ice until you need them.

When using shad up to 3 or 4 inches long, don't cut the bait into pieces. Fish them whole, but score the sides of each bait to release cat-attracting

The author's son, Matt, with a nice winter channel cat that couldn't resist a juicy shad cut-bait.

juices. Cut larger shad into three pieces—head, middle, and tail. I always start by using the middle or "gut" section. Shad guts definitely attract more channel cats than the flesh alone. When I have dozens of large shad, I use the guts alone, reserving the other parts for when my bait supply runs low.

One place to try coldkill fishing is in the rushing tailrace below a dam. Shad that die above a dam drift through the turbines, and many are sliced and diced in the process. Big channel cats are attracted by the resulting "chum" and often stack up like cordwood in the tailwater, gorging on the abundant shad pieces.

In this situation, I use a float-rig presentation, so the shad bait drifts through catfish holding areas in much the same way it would if drifting naturally in the current. The best such rig features a large sliding float. A bobber stop and plastic bead are placed on the line so the sliding float just beneath them will suspend the bait at the desired depth. Beneath the bobber, tie a 6/0 to 8/0 circle hook or octopus hook, then, if necessary, add several split shot to sink the bait.

Cast this rig as close as possible to the face of the dam, and allow it to drift with the current. I prefer a 12-foot surf rod/spinning reel combo, which allows longer casts and permits me to maneuver the rig so that it drifts through different areas where channel cats hold. I find it particularly effective to bring the rig into the slower-moving water in "grooves" between the dam gates. The bait will often stop momentarily in these spots, and if the coldkill bite is peaking, a channel cat is sure to strike when it does.

Blue Catfish

Spring Crayfish for Eating-Size Blues

Blue cats over 10 pounds are fish eaters. But younger, smaller blues—eating-size fish—take a wide variety of foods. Among their favorites are crayfish, and on many big bottomland rivers, spring floods allow blue cats to gorge on an abundance of mudbugs not available during other seasons.

Crayfish are abundant in bottomland hardwood forests, but during most of the year, they live on land and are inaccessible to catfish. During overflow periods, however, crayfish live in an aquatic environment, and catfish are drawn to them like kids to a candy store. Big blue cats rarely leave rivers to feed in flooded woods, but smaller blues do. They swim from rivers, bayous, and sloughs into the shallow water that now inundates many acres. They feed on crayfish here as long as the water is high enough to swim in, sometimes for several months.

In spring, blue cats often gorge on the bounty of terrestrial crayfish that becomes available when bottomland rivers flood adjacent woodlands.

Anglers should pay particular attention to the part of this phenomenon known as "the run-off." This occurs when a river "falls out of" a connected oxbow, usually in spring or early summer when overflow waters recede. When the water gets low enough, the only connections between an oxbow and its parent stream are small chutes or "run-outs" created by low points in the topography. All run-outs serve up extraordinary catfishing.

The best fishing in run-outs is during the few days before the river falls out of the lake. Water constricted in the run-outs increases in velocity. Crayfish are pulled by current into the rushing stream of water and adjacent areas. Catfish gather in great numbers to gorge on the resulting feast. Some hold near cover at the head of the run-out, in the lake. Others stay near the run-out's tail, where rushing water meets the river. All feed ravenously, and a crayfish bait worked through or along the run-out will be eaten quickly.

A sliding-float rig using a 4/0 to 5/0 baitholder hook works great here, with the bobber positioned so the bait floats just off the bottom. Cast above the run-out and let the rig drift back, or drift the rig through current in the run-out tail.

For successful run-out fishing, learn the river-gauge level at which the parent river will overflow into each oxbow. When gauge numbers are higher than this baseline, the river and oxbow are connected. When gauge numbers are lower than the "magic" number, the river and oxbow are separated. Run-off conditions exist when the river level is just slightly higher than the magic number, and it is during the few days when this occurs that run-out catfishing is at its best.

Summer's Herring Bite

Skipjack herring are common in many big rivers inhabited by blue cats. They comprise a major portion of the blue cat's diet in some areas, and many catfishermen use them for bait. They're easy to capture in cast nets, on sabiki rigs, or on small jigs or spoons.

Skipjacks are active baitfish, moving continuously in large schools. They're fish-eaters, with minnows, shad, and other small fishes among their favored foods. This fact makes them doubly attractive to blue cats, especially in late summer. Here's why.

In July and August, large schools of skipjacks churn the water's surface as they pursue young-of-the-year shad. You can see the fish swirling near the surface, with shad jumping about as they try to elude the skipjacks.

This activity usually occurs near dawn and dusk, frequently near creek mouths or at the junction of two rivers.

When surfacing skipjacks are sighted, scores of blue cats likely are lurking below. They're attracted not only by the prospect of a skipjack entrée, but also by the many dead and crippled shad left behind when skipjacks slash through a school. Sometimes striped or white bass join the feeding frenzy, too, working on skipjacks and shad alike. This increases the number of injured baitfish fluttering about, another drawing card for gluttonous blues.

For the died-in-the-wool blue cat angler, this is a setting like no other. A $\frac{1}{64}$- to $\frac{1}{32}$-ounce silver or white jig cast toward swirling fish will usually garner a strike from a skipjack that can be used for bait. Cut the skippie in small pieces, run a hook through one, then cast it toward the swirls and let it fall to hungry blues waiting below.

Keep your fishing rig as simple as possible for best results. All you need is a circle hook or octopus hook at the end of the line with nothing more than a split shot or two to carry it down.

Fishing a skipjack herring cut-bait produced this nice Mississippi River blue cat for the author. BILL DANCE

Drift-Fishing Cut-Bait for Autumn Blues

Blue catfish are nomadic in autumn, following baitfish schools and seeking comfort zones. They're scattered and difficult to pinpoint, which frustrates many anglers. You can sit on the bank and try to catch a mess, but drift-fishing works better. This is an active approach to catfishing that can make your catch rate soar, and it's a good way to target trophy fish.

Autumn blues may roam around bottom channels, humps, depressions, or other readily identifiable structures. A serious look at a lake contour map and a quick check of prominent bottom changes with a fish-finder can help you locate them.

Many cat men use a special float rig for drift-fishing. The main line is run through the eye of a sinker (usually a pencil weight or bell sinker), and a barrel swivel is tied below it to keep the weight from sliding down.

Drift-fishing is an excellent way to locate and catch fall blue cats roaming with schools of baitfish.

A 12- to 18-inch leader is then tied to the lower eye of the swivel. A small float is placed in the middle of the leader, and a 5/0 to 8/0 wide-gap circle hook is tied at the end and baited. The float suspends the baited hook above bottom to prevent snags.

Shad or herring cut-baits are widely considered the best drift-fishing baits, and where permitted, up to eight rods may be used. Position the rods in rod holders, then let the wind carry the boat across the channel-edge flats where fish are holding, or use a trolling motor to maneuver over structures likely to hold blues.

Proper speed is important when drift-fishing, but there's no magic formula for determining what speed is best under a given set of conditions. On some days, you may have to inch your boat along to get strikes. On other days you'll have to troll so fast you'll wonder how catfish could possibly catch your bait. And when you find the productive speed, you must maintain it, even when wind and current push your boat ahead or drive it back.

Winter Fishing on Shallow Mussel Beds

Freshwater mussels attract winter blue cats like rabbits to a garden patch. Mussels live in bottom colonies called "beds," each containing thousands of these mollusks. Cats in cold water visit the beds repeatedly because they can gorge here day after day with little expenditure of energy.

The inch-long Asiatic clam, now common in many North American lakes and rivers, is a special favorite for catfish, but they also relish native mussels—especially smaller varieties like lilliputs, wartybacks, and deertoes. Blue cats also gorge on zebra mussels, the noxious invaders that have colonized many U.S. waters.

Shell and all is eaten, regardless of the mussel species. Digestive juices kill the mussel, the shell opens, the flesh inside is digested, and then the shell is passed by the fish. Some catfish have so many shells in their belly that they rattle like maracas.

Blue cats feed on many varieties of mussels in winter.

To find mussel beds, search near shore in 1 to 6 feet of water. They can be pinpointed by sight during low-water periods, or you can find them by moving parallel to shore and probing the bottom with a pole. The shells produce a distinctive crunching sound when the pole hits them.

An egg-sinker rig with a sturdy 3/0 to 5/0 wide-gap circle hook works great here. Cast to a likely spot and allow the rig to sit for up to fifteen minutes. If no bite is forthcoming, move to another portion of the shell bed and try again. Good enticements include inch-square chunks of shad, herring, or hot dogs, which are the same size as the mussels most catfish eat. The mussels themselves need not be used, and unless you are an expert at distinguishing various species you should avoid them because many are protected species.

A big ball of night crawlers was an irresistible enticement for this jumbo flathead.

Flathead Catfish

A Ball of Crawlers for Spring

In spring, when heavy rains cause rivers and lakes to rise and become muddy, flatheads go on a run-and-gun feeding spree. Some anglers believe they are hungry after a winter on lean rations, and the sudden influx of food animals washed into the water by warm rain stimulates feeding activity. Others believe the spawning urge draws the fish together, and they feed ravenously to fatten up before egg-laying and nesting. Whatever the case, this is a boon time for flathead fans. No better situation exists for catching flatheads in numbers.

Night crawlers are among the many foods flatheads are eating this time of year. Although bigger, older cats tend to feed almost exclusively on fish, they are opportunistic to some extent, and will gorge on big worms washed into the water by spring rains.

To catch these cats, try this specialized setup. First, place a 1- to 2-ounce egg sinker on your main line, and below this tie a barrel swivel. To the other eye of the swivel, tie a 3-foot leader with an 8/0 to 12/0 wide-gap circle hook on one end. Bait the hook with as many night crawlers as you can impale upon it. Leave the ends of the worms dangling loosely. You want as many loose ends as possible, and you want to put enough worms on the hook to create a wad the size of a tennis ball. When done, cast the worm-ball to a root wad or some other structure where you think a flathead might be.

Small fish—sunfish, suckers, little catfish—will nibble the ends of the worms. A big flathead nearby will watch the little fish, and if nothing disturbs the little ones, Ol' Jumbo knows it's safe to go out and eat. When you notice the nibbling stop, that means the small fish are fleeing as the big cat approaches. This is the point when you should prepare for a strike.

Many anglers have trouble with this technique. If the little fish stop nibbling, a person may think their bait is gone, so they reel in and check it. More than likely, plenty of worms are still on the hook. But some anglers can't stand the suspense, so they retrieve the worm-ball when the little bites stop, and the whole process must be repeated—casting, waiting on the little fish to start eating, waiting while the big fish watches for the little fish, and so forth. You'll be more successful if you can resist the temptation to disturb the bait when it's on the bottom. Leave it out there and wait, and when the nibbling stops, get ready to cross the eyes on a big flathead.

Sunfish baits work great when flatheads are feeding in the shallows during summer.

Summer Sunfish

Wherever flathead catfish are found, sunfish such as bluegills, redears, green sunfish, pumpkinseeds, and longear sunfish are sure to be. Not surprisingly, flatheads, being fish-eaters, love a meal of these usually abundant panfish. In some waters, sunfish are the number-one component of the flathead's diet.

Summer flatheads tend to hole up in deepwater haunts during the day and come out at night to feed in shallows. Sunfish usually stay in relatively shallow water, and many are still nesting along the shoreline in this season. That makes them prime targets for prowling flatheads and excellent baits for summer anglers.

Check local regulations to learn any restrictions regarding sunfish baits, and then collect those species and sizes you're allowed to use. In some areas, you may be able to use a seine or fish trap to catch sunfish in quantity, but catching them on hook and line can be fun in its own right.

If you want to exclude small flatheads from your catch and zero in on trophies, use the biggest sunfish the law allows. For giant flatheads, fish 50 pounds and up, this may mean a bait that weighs 8 ounces to 1 pound or more. It's tough to cast a bait that size, but you don't have to. Rig it up, and then use a boat to place it right where you want it. For flathead fishing at night, this usually is in shallow water not far from thick woody cover such as a logjam, treetop, brush, or other such feature.

Although it takes a bit more time to prepare than other rigs, the paternoster rig is ideal for this situation. This European-style setup was created especially for fishing big fish baits. The sinker anchors the rig while the baitfish struggles enticingly above the bottom.

Place the rig by casting or using a boat, then let it sit. You don't want to move the bait too often. Trophy-class flatheads are rare creatures, even in the best waters, so it may be necessary to leave the bait in one spot for an hour or more until a hungry, cruising heavyweight can find it.

Carp and Goldfish for Autumn's Drift-Pile Flatheads

Flatheads love dense woody cover. One such place where you'll find them in fall is a drift pile, or log raft. These platforms of floating logs and debris form in big-river backwaters during high water. As the river rises and current velocity increases, the main current presses against the seam of more quiet water in the backwater and causes it to swirl like a gigantic whirlpool. Logs and other woody debris in the river are pulled into the eddy and form floating platforms sometimes 100 yards or more across. These structures attract many types of baitfish that nibble food off the logs, and the baitfish in turn attract flatheads.

Various types of carp—common carp, bigheads, silver carp, and others—are common in big rivers where flatheads are found, and they, like other fish, are attracted to drift piles. When they can be obtained alive (often from a commercial fisherman or caught on hook and line), carp of the right size, 6 to 12 inches long, make great baits for drift-pile flatheads.

Big goldfish baits worked beneath drift piles often roust out big hungry flatheads.

They're hardy on the hook and able to survive better than other baitfish in the maelstrom of debris. If carp aren't available, goldfish may be. Bait dealers often carry them, and in waters where it's legal to use them, goldfish are popular flathead enticements well-suited for fishing drift piles.

To fish a drift pile, anchor your boat to one side, or find a bankfishing spot with access to the outer edges of the logs. Flatheads often hold beneath central portions of a drift pile, but it's much easier to fish the edges where flatheads also feed. Present your baitfish on an egg-sinker rig, but don't use an overly large sinker. You want the eddy to grab your rig and pull it under the outer edge of the drift pile. Use just enough weight to carry the bait slowly to the bottom in whatever current is present. Then, after casting, hold your rod tip high and strip line manually from your reel, guiding your rig beneath the rotating maze of logs. If a bite hasn't come by the time your line is caught by a piece of driftwood, move it and try again. If flatheads are present, they'll usually bite within minutes after your bait touches bottom.

Winter Flatheads on Lures and Lure Combos

Most veteran flathead anglers begin fishing when water temperatures warm into the 60-degree range in spring, and they put away their tackle when water temperatures cool below 50 degrees in fall. The reason for this is simple. Flatheads become increasingly inactive when the water temperature falls below 50 degrees. And their winter lethargy makes them hard to catch.

Flatheads feed very seldom in cold, winter water, but can sometimes be enticed if anglers use the right tactics.

In rivers, winter flatheads congregate in deep holes with flat, sandy, silt-free bottoms and some form of shelter from current. Most hide behind rocks, logs, or other features that break the current, and sometimes the fish lay one behind another, their bodies actually touching. The numbers of flatheads in these wintering holes can be astounding. A study in the upper Mississippi River, for example, found the population on one 300-yard stretch of river bottom varied from about 250 per acre to as high as 2,350 per acre.

Establishing a reliable winter pattern for river flatheads has been difficult because, even though hundreds of flatheads may be found in a small area, these cold-water fish feed very little. In recent years, however, some hardcore flathead fanatics have reported success by first pinpointing flathead aggregations with sonar, then working a bait right in front of the fish using a slow, vertical presentation. Two baits being used with some success—to the surprise of many veteran cat men—are a 3- to 5-inch, soft-plastic shad imitation such as the Mister Twister Sassy Shad and a ¼- to ⅛-ounce jig tipped with a 4- to 6-inch shiner.

Winter flathead fishing is tough, period. But if you have an itch to try it, you may want to give these tactics a try. Work the lure or jig/shiner combo vertically over a rocky bottom, fishing straight down to minimize hang-ups. Pay close attention to your business, and if anything feels amiss—if the bait stops short of where you think the bottom should be when you raise it, for example, or if your line twitches in a way it hasn't been doing—set the hook. Sometimes a cold-water flathead will really whack your rig when you put it in front of its nose, but just as often the cat will sort of yawn it in, and the strike will be as light as that of a crappie.

CHAPTER TEN

Tactics of the Masters

The best way to learn new catfishing tricks is to pick the brains of your catfishing friends. Every hardcore angler has special tricks and tactics no one else seems to know.

Some of our country's best catfishermen have been kind enough to share their fishing expertise with me, and the information these masters of the sport provided can help you be a better angler, too.

Big River Flatheads: James Patterson

Flathead catfish have been stocked in thousands of man-made lakes and ponds across the country. They also are native to many natural lakes and small streams. But flatheads evolved in the currents of our largest rivers, and it's in these waters that they reach their greatest numbers and largest size. The trophy hunter who understands the how, where, and when of targeting these cats in big-river environs can enjoy first-rate angling for a sportfish that sometimes weighs more than 100 pounds.

James Patterson of Bartlett, Tennessee, knows this how, where, and when better than most folks. The proprietor of Mississippi River Guide Service, he's on "The Father of Waters" at Memphis hundreds of days each year, and often as not, it's trophy flatheads he's targeting.

"The flathead has a mystique all its own," Patterson says. "And part of that mystique relates to the difficulty of catching it. Even in waters like the Mississippi River where flatheads are common, locating trophy-class specimens is not easy. In a big-river environment, water levels and water clarity are ever-changing, and the location of prime fishing spots is unpredictable day in and day out."

Despite their unpredictability, giant flatheads fall for Patterson's fishing tactics on a regular basis. And the proven mix of tactics he uses can be employed by other big-river catfishermen with a high expectation of success.

How

The first lesson in the basics of big-river flathead fishing is how to select the right fishing gear. Using the proper rods, reels, line, terminal tackle, and bait is imperative for success. There are many options to consider, but Patterson says some tackle items have qualities that make them better for flathead fishing than others.

Take rods, for example. When pursuing giant tackle-busting flatheads, a heavy action might seem best. But Patterson's experience has shown lighter may be better.

"I use Quantum Big Cat rods in medium action," he reports. "The medium action is the lightest action of all the Big Cat rods, but I prefer these rods because they have a light tip that prevents the fish from feeling the rod, plus enough butt strength to pull a big fish up."

Catfish guide James Patterson of Bartlett, Tennessee, uses specialized tactics to catch big-river flatheads.

Each of Patterson's rods is paired with a Quantum Iron IR410C baitcasting reel spooled with 65-pound-test Stren Super Braid. To this, he usually attaches one of two basic flathead rigs: a three-way-swivel rig or a basic float rig.

To make the three-way-swivel rig, "I use leaders of Stren Magnaflex monofilament in a bright fluorescent green color," Patterson notes. "The 24- to 32-inch hook leader is 50-pound-test mono. The 6- to 10-inch sinker leader is 30-pound-test. I use Eagle Claw L-141 Kahle hooks with a Black Platinum finish, usually in the 7/0 size. Sometimes larger hooks are needed when using large baits. [Patterson's flathead baits often weigh half a pound or more.] To complete the rig, the two leaders and the main line are each tied to a separate eye on a large three-way swivel."

Sinker size and type varies according to the amount of current and the area being fished, but in most situations, Patterson uses a 3- or 4-ounce bank sinker.

"I sometimes add a small Styrofoam float onto my hook leader to float the live bait off the bottom," he says. "This is pegged a few inches above the hook."

Patterson's float rig consists of five basic components: a big balsa or Styrofoam slip float that will suspend an 8-ounce bait; a bobber stop; a ½- to 1-ounce egg sinker; a sturdy barrel swivel and a 7/0 Kahle hook. The bobber stop goes on the line first and is positioned so when the float abuts it, the bait will suspend about a foot above the bottom. Next the float is added and below it the egg sinker and then the barrel swivel. Patterson then ties the 24-inch hook leader to the swivel.

Big flatheads scavenge very little, preferring live food, especially fish and crustaceans.

"I use baits such as shad, goldfish, river shrimp, small bighead carp, small grass carp, small buffalo, bream, and river minnows," Patterson says. "These are caught with a cast net, hook and bait, or with the aid of minnow/shrimp traps.

"Any good live bait native to the river will work," he notes. "I hook the shrimp through the tail and leave the barb sticking out. Live fish are hooked through the lips when in current because strong current can open the baitfish's gill flaps and kill it if it's hooked behind the dorsal fin. When fishing slack water, however, I hook the baitfish behind the dorsal fin."

When submerged, buckled revetment like this provides shelter for flatheads.

Where

The locales where Patterson seeks big-river flatheads are of three basic types: (1) cavities and rotating current areas that form in or near cuts in shoreline revetment and/or riprap; (2) upstream edges of rock jetties or dikes; and (3) bottom troughs along bluff banks with woody cover.

The first type of hotspot can be found on big-river navigation systems maintained by government agencies such as the U.S. Army Corps of Engineers. To stabilize the river banks and prevent erosion, bulldozers are used to smooth the shoreline, then the soil is covered with concrete matting called revetment. The revetment may be covered with a layer of large limestone rocks (riprap) to further stabilize it.

Circular areas of rotating current that resemble gigantic, slow-moving whirlpools often form where the river races past "cuts" formed when fast-moving water erodes soil beneath the revetment. As the undercut increases in size, the concrete/rock superstructure eventually collapses and sinks, creating a deep hole adjacent the bank.

"I like to fish slow or rotating current areas around these cuts," Patterson says. "Some of these rotating currents are no bigger than a large automobile; others may be as large as a football field. It all depends on the depth and length of the cut. No matter what their size, though, all such areas tend to hold big flatheads."

It's possible to catch a flathead in one of these pools simply by anchoring upstream, casting a float rig or three-way-swivel rig into the rotating water, and waiting for a bite. But chances of a trophy catch increase if the angler can pinpoint a large hole that has formed beneath buckled revetment. Giant flatheads love the security of these dark cavities, and anglers who use a "finesse" presentation to put the bait right in front of the fish often find themselves battling a trophy-class cat.

"A good depthfinder is essential for finding these underwater houses," says Patterson. "I usually start downstream and troll slowly upstream parallel to the bank, watching the screen for the ups and downs of these buckled-up revetment slabs. When I find a hole and feel like the boat is directly over it,

I pick out a reference spot on the bank. Then I motor upstream and anchor the boat casting distance away from the hole. I typically use a float rig set 4 to 6 feet deep for this type of fishing because the revetment houses are small, and precise location is mandatory for success. I cast directly over the hole, let the rig settle, and wait for a hit. If I haven't had a bite after fifteen to twenty minutes, I troll up the bank until I find another likely spot and anchor again. I continue doing this, working my way upstream and fishing first one hole and then another."

If strong wind and/or current make it difficult to properly position and hold the boat, Patterson may beach his craft and walk the bank to present a live bait in a similar manner.

"You have to be extremely stealthy to fish this way," he notes. "Flatheads, like all cats, have very sensitive hearing, making it hard to slip down the rock bank without being detected. But this tactic may earn you a bite if you can't fish the hole any other way."

Rock jetties or dikes are another type of structure where a "get out of the boat and walk" presentation is useful. The best extend from bank to bank, usually behind islands.

Flatheads are attracted to the jetties by the promise of a shad dinner. In summer, when the river gets low enough, the water between two jetties may form a lake that clears quickly as mud and sediment settle to the bottom. Large algae blooms occur in the clear water, and the algae attract feeding shad. The schools of shad attract hungry catfish.

"Flatheads typically hold on the upstream side of these rock formations," says Patterson. "And presenting a live shad under a cork is a surefire way to catch them. Work the top side of the dike quietly and slowly from bank to bank, paying particular attention to places where water runs through rocks in the dike or over low spots. These areas have some current, and cats will hold nearby waiting to ambush the baitfish."

Another summer hotspot in big rivers is where a steep mud bank, slow current, and timber combine to create an area attractive to flatheads. Cats visit these areas in spring looking for spawning sites in protected cavities and undercuts in the woody cover, and may remain here or revisit the area in other seasons to feed on baitfish and crustaceans.

"I look for bluff banks with timber or old stumps sticking up," Patterson states. "These are excellent fishing spots, particularly those on the downstream side of shallow sandbars where the current is slow and

baitfish stack up. These banks often drop off into troughs of water that are more than 20 feet deep just 40 feet offshore. The troughs typically run parallel to the bank, and they're great features for cats. Flatheads run the troughs most of the year, depending on the water level and current speed. And you can catch them by working one of the two basic rigs in and around the cover."

When

Flatheads are caught year-round in portions of their range, including that stretch of the Mississippi River where James Patterson usually fishes. For this cat man, however, summer is the season for flatheads, and night time is the right time.

"Flatheads frequent shallow water throughout summer," he says. "And that makes them easier to target. In big rivers like the Mississippi, depths of 100 feet or more are not rare. But in summer, even though the water temperature may reach 80 degrees or more, the flatheads usually are in less than 20 feet of water."

Feeding activity peaks at night.

"Summer flatheads definitely bite better after dark or at the first part of the sunrise or sunset," Patterson notes. "So fish at night or near dawn and dusk for the best chance of success."

But in the end, Patterson says the best time to fish for flatheads is whenever you can go.

"The flathead is the king of big rivers," he says of his beloved cat. "I sometimes hear people call it 'mud cat,' but I assure you it doesn't deserve that title like a lowly bullhead. The flathead is a true predator, a sprinter that can run down the fastest fish. It has a monstrous mouth and can swallow a fish a fourth of its size. This fellow can give you one of the best fights of any catfish, and he is by far the finest table fare of all the cats.

"Patience is a virtue you must have to catch flatheads consistently," he concludes. "It's never easy. But when fishing big rivers for this incredible fish, the next flathead you tie into could be a 50- or 60-pounder, maybe even bigger. That makes all the extra effort worthwhile."

Amen to that.

How to Get a Cat Out of a Tree: Denny Halgren

If you want to catch a cat, look in a tree. As often as not, you'll find one.

The cat of which I speak is not the furry feline that rubs against your legs or purrs in your lap, of course. I'm talking about hairless, aquatic kitties like the channel cat. This species likes protected homesites in inundated trees. And if you can pinpoint trees from which they're ambushing prey, you can entice these pole-bending tabbies with treats they can't resist.

My friend Denny Halgren, a Dixon, Illinois, catfish guide, likes catching cats in trees—channel cats, in particular. Some folks who see him fishing for these tree-loving river kitties think he's in trouble. Often, his boat is smack-dab on top of a big tree laid over in the water. He might be in the boat, but more likely, he'll be standing on the tree with a rod and reel.

Halgren calls this technique "crashin' and thrashin'," and with good reason. First, you "crash" your boat into big timber, the only effective means for reaching those hard-to-get-at catfish hotspots other anglers wouldn't dare fish. Next, you drop a bait into the swirling water at just the right spot. Then, if all goes well, and a catfish is there (one usually is), you experience the thrashin' part. The fish nabs the bait, you set the hook, and you try to hoss a big catfish out of its hidey-hole.

"One day I decided to try something different," Halgren says, explaining how he discovered this overlooked catfishing tactic. "I crawled out on top of a big tree instead of casting out beside it. The water was flowing just right to create a monster boil on the downstream side. I dropped a bait into the boil and got bit. And I pulled a dandy channel cat out of that hole. When I fished other trees in the same way, I caught more channel cats.

"After I bought I boat, I continued fishing these same kinds of spots. The boat gave me more mobility. I could fish dozens of trees each time out, instead of just a few. And the more I fished, the more I learned. Now, years later, I've learned enough to teach others this great method for catching big channel cats."

The key, Halgren says, is learning to pinpoint the exact spot where a big cat is likely to be. That spot will have two primary components: a big tree and a big boil.

"The ideal place," he says, "is where current has undercut a tree and caused it to topple over into the water. At least part of the tree must be in shallow water—2 to 3 feet deep—and there must be at least moderate

current coming across the tree. When the right amount of current is present, the biggest, most territorial catfish centralize. In other words, the current causes them to hold in very specific spots where they can easily grab food carried in the current. Without proper current, the fish could be anywhere and are difficult to pinpoint. When the current is right, you can find them every time."

Prime locales rarely consist of more than one tree or trees lying parallel to the bank. When scouting a river, anglers should look for a single fallen tree positioned perpendicular to the bank, with the root end still close to shore in shallow water.

"In the best spots, current washes underneath the trunk of the tree in shallow water, and creates a channel," Halgren says. "As the water goes through that channel, it's funneled through to the downstream side of the tree and creates a big boil. Right in that boil is where you want to fish. You may catch smaller catfish in other spots around the perimeter of the tree. But the biggest cat on that piece of cover will almost always be in the biggest boil."

A good stretch of river may encompass dozens of locations exhibiting these features when water levels are right. Some almost always hold big catfish. Others aren't as productive. If you fish the same stretch frequently, you'll learn which are which and can zero in on the honeyholes without wasting time at substandard locales.

"I'm not sure why these boils attract big catfish," says Halgren. "But they do. You'll seldom catch a small fish in a place like I've described. These are the biggest cats in that stretch of water, and they're not resting in these boils, they're actively feeding. That's a prime feeding spot, so that big fish makes it his territory. And the only thing that will run him out is a bigger fish. Consequently, big cats are what you'll catch."

The crashin' part of this technique isn't as dangerous as it sounds. You don't actually have to crash your boat into a tree, although Halgren has been known to do just that.

"I've hit the brush too fast and raised my boat completely out of the water," he says. "I've been knocked out of the boat, had minor cuts and abrasions, lost several pairs of glasses, and even speared my boat into the bank, filling it up with dirt. The point is, be careful. Don't move too fast when trying to get your boat positioned."

Ideally, after spotting a good tree/boil location, the boat operator slows the boat and allows it to slide gently onto the tree trunk or into the tree's branches. When it's done properly, the boat will catch and hold, and the fisherman will be able to drop his bait into the boil.

"You may have to crash your boat right up on top of the tree," Halgren notes. "You must be positioned so you can drop your bait straight down into the largest boil on the downstream side of the trunk. Sometimes it's simply a matter of floating your boat sideways along the tree and dropping a bait in. If I can't do it any other way, I'll put on my life jacket and climb out of the boat and up on the tree to fish. It's important to drop your bait straight down, because this allows you to fight the fish straight up, increasing your chances of getting it out."

Some anglers try anchoring upstream and fishing the perimeter of the tree, thinking the bait will draw a catfish out of its hiding place. Halgren says this may be true for smaller catfish, but big cats tend to hold tight to the cover, requiring a drop-it-on-their-nose presentation.

"If you're fishing the edges, you're not going to get the biggest catfish in there," he states emphatically. "There's no reason for that fish to leave his sanctuary. He has everything he wants. He can sit and wait for the food to come to him.

"What's surprising to most anglers is that riding your boat up on that tree only rarely spooks the fish out. The big cats just don't spook, so you can move right in on top of them."

When fishing woody cover, Halgren says that it's important to use bait that triggers quick hits from feeding fish. His favorite is a commercial cheese-flavored dip bait, JoJo's Pole Snatcher made by Cat Tracker Bait Company.

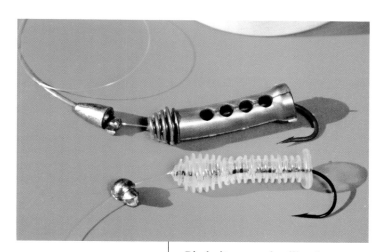

Dip bait worm rigs like these are used by cat expert Denny Halgren to tempt big channel cats in boils around downed trees.

"There's no flour in this bait," he says, "so the bait doesn't slough off. If that happens, the catfish will eat the bait but won't get your hook. You can't catch him that way. The Cat Tracker bait stays on the worm where it's needed."

The "worm" Halgren refers to is a Cat Tracker Tubie 2000 or Cat Tracker Egg Worm. These special-made, soft-plastic baits are ribbed so the dip bait clings when the worm is pushed into it. The Egg Worm comes prerigged with a 2-foot section of 20-pound-test mono run through the worm and tied to a small treble hook that fits snuggly against the tail end. The Tubie 2000 is made to be rigged by the angler.

Halgren uses single 2/0 or 3/0 Tru-Turn hooks on both rigs—catfish hooks with the Tubie 2000 and worm hooks with the Egg Worm. The rig is tied to his main line—20-pound Stren mono—with a ¼-ounce split shot or bullet sinker on the line above the worm. When using a bullet sinker, place a split shot below it to peg it on the line.

"If I'm dropping baits into a spot with a lot of branches, I slide the weight down so it almost touches the top of the worm," Halgren says. "If the boil is behind the trunk and pretty free of obstruction, I slide the weight up above the worm about 6 inches. This type of rig is simple and ideal for fishing in these situations. In 4 to 5 mph current, the bait will stay on about 45 minutes."

Halgren prefers a 6- to 7½-foot, medium heavy to heavy action Aurora Pro Cat Series II rod paired with Aurora's Suntech 2 ST2400 baitcasting reel.

"I carry rods of various lengths," he notes. "Sometimes a 6-footer is too short to reach the boil and drop a bait straight down. A 7½ may be too long. You need to have a choice."

Halgren rarely fishes a spot longer than ten minutes.

"Catfish usually bite quickly when you use this bait and rig in this situation," he says. "I drop the rig in the boil, then leave it. You can't move the bait, even if you think it's hung. Chances are, you'll get a hit right away. If not, wait for up to ten minutes. If you don't have a catfish by then, it's time to move and try another spot."

Catching more than one jumbo catfish at each fishing spot happens only rarely. "When you catch one, you might as well head for another tree," Halgren says.

Flathead catfish love woody cover, but channel cats comprise most of Halgren's catch.

"This tactic produces big channel cats, from 4 to 12 pounds. Even though they're hefty cats, you can set the hook, keep a tight line, and get them out. Get them up and let them thrash at the top of the water. That way they won't get wrapped up, and you can get them out.

"Flatheads are another story altogether. You can't hoist a big flathead to the surface in a treetop. With those guys, it's an entirely different scenario. You'll *hook* plenty of flatheads, but most of the fish you *catch* will be channel cats."

Of course, getting a cat out of a tree is never easy, whether it has fur or fins. You may get scratched. You could fall. You have to be brave—some say crazy—to try. But if you're brave enough, or crazy enough, to fish where other anglers won't, big cats will be your prize. Fishing in trees is a surefire method for catching cats.

King Cats: Phil King

In the 1950s, Cecil Parris put Savannah, Tennessee, on the map. Parris ran a toy gun business, and his return packages kept getting sent to that other Savannah in Georgia. So he went to the local post office and convinced them to add "Catfish Capital of the World" to the postmark used to cancel mail. The title stuck, and it's deserved today as much as it was fifty years ago. Nearby Pickwick Lake, a 43,100-acre Tennessee River impoundment, provides blue-ribbon angling for jumbo blue, channel, and flathead catfish.

Corinth, Mississippi, catfish guide Phil King has targeted cats in

Pickwick Lake and other Tennessee River impoundments for more than a quarter century, and he's good at what he does. He and partner Stacey Thompson have made a name for themselves in the catfish tournament world with championships in the Cabela's King Kat Classic, the World Championship of Catfishing, Cat Masters USA, and many more. King also has claimed more than twenty big fish titles throughout his tournament career.

"I fish often on Pickwick from the Mississippi/Alabama state line to Pickwick Dam," he says. "Catfishing is good to excellent eleven months of the year, with January being the slowest."

Vertical Trolling for Blue and Channel Catfish

I've had the pleasure of fishing with King, who taught me several catfishing tactics anyone can apply successfully on almost any big river.

The first method, vertical trolling, is used primarily to catch blue and channel catfish. It employs the big-river finesse rig developed by King himself (see chapter six). The rig is baited with either a big bloody chunk of fresh chicken liver or what King describes as a "catfish sandwich." The latter is simply the innards of a big skipjack herring sandwiched between two side fillets from the same baitfish.

Catfishing pro Phil King of Corinth, Mississippi, hoists a giant blue cat taken in the Tennessee River system where he guides. PHIL KING

"For this tactic, I prefer using Cabela's 8-foot or 9-foot King Kat rod, or the 7-foot, 6-inch Signature rods," King notes. "All three have a light tip to detect even the slightest bite.

"This method works well in deep-water lakes and rivers in low or no current conditions," he continues. "Placing the rods in rod holders, I can cover a path 20 feet wide or more out of my boat. I use a different bait on each rod, covering different depths of the water column until I find the depth where active fish are biting. I can fish close to the bottom or catch suspended cats I see on the depthfinder."

Proper trolling speed is critical when using this tactic. The baits should hang vertically, as the name of this technique implies. King uses a trolling motor to move the boat and tries to maintain a speed that does not exceed 0.5 mile per hour.

"This method worked well for Stacey Thompson and me in the 2003 King Kat Classic," King said. "It allowed us to have one of our best days ever tournament fishing—seven catfish weighing a whopping 187 pounds."

King uses the same rig and baits to fish for blues, flatheads, and channel cats in deep river holes, some dropping below 70 feet. He starts at the head of a hole and drifts through, after the bait rig has been lowered to the bottom. Most cats hold beside river-bottom timber and rocks, which "telegraph" signals through the braided line to the angler above. The angler must be attentive at all times, raising and lowering the rod tip so he maintains "feel" with the rig below and keeps it bouncing across the pieces of cover and structure without hanging.

While drifting, King watches a fish-finder for signals indicating cats holding near structures below. If he spies good fish that fail to take the bait on the first drift, he may drift through the hole again, targeting those spots once more that appeared to hold catfish.

For the big-river angler hoping to catch numbers of cats with an occasional trophy-class fish in the mix, this is a superb technique that's easy to learn. King has used it to catch blues and flatheads weighing up to 50 pounds.

Crankbaits for Flatheads

The portion of the Tennessee River King fishes harbors good numbers of big flatheads, too, and he sometimes fishes for these brutes.

"Flatheads will hang in and around the same spots blues will," he says. "But they like to have something to relate to such as bridge structures, deep ledges with rock or logs, or the tailwaters of hydroelectric dams. You can catch them during daylight hours by drifting or from an anchored boat. Typically, flatheads prefer live baits, but they also will hit strips of cut-bait that resemble injured live baits when the strips move in the current."

In spring, when newly hatched shad and skipjack herring migrate to the dams, King looks for flatheads that move in to feed on these baitfish. During this time of year, he says, "You can catch flatheads below the dams in the edge of the current flow or in slow-moving current."

In summer, many flatheads spawn in cavities that form in the riprapped banks along many man-made lakes and waterways. According to King, the flatheads generally stay in these areas after spawning.

"The technique for catching these fish is trolling crankbaits that will dive to the bottom where the riprap stops," he notes. "The flatheads wallow out holes to spawn in where the mud meets the rocks. I use deep-diving crankbaits and a trolling motor that will drive the lures down to the bottom. When the lures start hitting bottom, I slow the trolling motor and allow the lures to skim the bottom. If a flathead is in the area, it will come up and smash the crankbait. Troll two to four rods with lures of different colors, and when the catfish show a preference for one color or another, rig all your rods with that particular color. Natural shad, blue-back shad, bright orange, and green work well for me."

King enjoys teaching anglers to catch catfish and takes pride in the fact that many come back to fish with him again and again.

Lures aren't often used for catfishing, but shadlike crankbaits can be dynamite on summer flatheads.

"One of the most satisfying things about being a guide," he says, "is when one of my clients catches their biggest catfish ever or tells me that they had the best day of fishing ever. These tactics help me accomplish that."

They can help you catch big cats, too.

Tidewater Tactics: Roger Aziz and Barry Mullin

Many catfishermen are surprised to learn that catfish—particularly blue cats and white cats—are abundant in the somewhat salty, brackish water of many coastal rivers and marshes from New England to the Gulf Coast states. Those willing to learn the tactics needed to catch catfish in these environs can open up a whole new realm of opportunities.

Understanding Tidewater Rivers

Water conditions in tidewater rivers change constantly because of the moon's gravitational pull on the Earth. The water level fluctuates several feet each day, the river's flow changes direction every 6½ hours, and current velocity varies enormously depending on moon phase, the distance from the river's mouth, and the amount of runoff. Savvy tidewater anglers pay close attention to tide tables, which appear daily in local newspapers, to plan their catfishing excursions. These show when high and low tides will occur in different spots on tidal rivers.

During a midsummer period of high flow and a full moon, a tidewater river has an upstream current during an incoming tide that's nearly as strong as the downstream current during an outgoing tide. With the same moon phase in early spring, however, the river will seem almost calm on an incoming tide. When the tide goes out, the current becomes much swifter, and fishing is more difficult. An angler's fishing success will improve if he studies such variations and learns when to expect certain conditions. Above the first dam or the fall line, the river is not influenced with tides.

White Cats in Coastal Rivers

White catfish range from California to Florida, but despite being widespread, and abundant in many waters, these fish largely are ignored. That's not the case in southern New England, however. In the waters of Massachusetts, New Hampshire, Rhode Island, and Connecticut, white cats often are the best thing going. Channel catfish inhabit this region, too, but in most areas, white cats are more abundant and catchable. Bullheads also swim in local waters, but they don't reach sizes that endear them to hardcore catfishing fanatics. There are no flatheads or blues within hundreds of miles. That leaves white cats as the fish of choice for many anglers.

Northeast anglers are especially fond of white cats because they thrive in the brackish water of coastal rivers where other cats are absent. They sometimes live in half-strength seawater, right at the mouth of major rivers. Catching them isn't always easy, however. For consistent success, one must possess a thorough knowledge of tidewater rivers and fishing tactics that work best.

Roger Aziz Jr. of Methuen, Massachusetts, has fished for catfish in the tidewater rivers of his home state since boyhood. He remembers a time years ago when he could catch scores of 4- to 7-pound white cats in the Merrimack River, a large tidewater stream flowing through parts of eastern New Hampshire and northeastern Massachusetts. He also remembers the dramatic decline of white cat numbers in the mid-1980s.

"At one time industrial factories lined both banks of the Merrimack," Aziz says. "The river was dirty, polluted, but there were lots of big white cats, and I was catching six or seven in the 5- to 7-pound range every time I went fishing. Around the mid-1980s, a virus killed off many bottom-dwelling fish, including many catfish and carp. They lay by the hundreds, dead against the shore. Catfishing tapered off from then on."

The river is cleaner now, and white cats are making a comeback.

"It's still difficult to catch a 5-pounder," says Aziz. "But the numbers are picking up. It's not unusual to catch fifteen to twenty whites a night weighing 1 to 2 pounds each. And eventually, I think we'll be catching much larger fish. Those of us who are serious about our catfishing don't kill any white cats. And other people are starting to follow our example, practicing catch and release. Catfishing is improving."

Aziz ranks among the country's top white cat anglers and has the credentials to prove it. He's caught several world line-class records, and the techniques he uses to catch the big ones from the Merrimack can work for other anglers, too.

"The best fishing in the Merrimack is the tidal water between Haverhill and Newburyport, about 20 miles of river," Aziz reports. "The white cats here are current lovers. The only place you'll catch them is in the current. I wait for the tide to peak, and as the water starts to go back out, that's when I fish. You can catch whites when the current's coming up, but they're more spread out then. The best fishing is on an outgoing tide."

Aziz targets rocky stretches of river, the same areas frequented by striped bass and smallmouths. In upstream reaches of the 20-mile pool, he finds most whites in deeper holes. When fishing closer to the river's mouth, he targets white cats holding around bridge abutments. He often fishes from shore using a 12-foot rod that allows a good long-distance hookset for taking cats off the bottom. When fishing from a boat, he prefers a 7-foot rod. Big spinning reels and 6- to 14-pound-test mono complete the outfits.

"My favorite rig uses a 2- to 3-ounce bass-casting sinker, or a no-roll sinker that I mold myself with a swivel in the top," Aziz notes. "A black rubber bead is placed between the sinker and a 3/0 Kahle hook. I fish this right on the bottom, letting the weight ride right against the hook. The sinker lays flat on the bottom, and the bait rides a few inches above it."

The baits Aziz uses are 1-inch chunks of cut shad or herring and, often, strips of bacon.

"Bacon works best in spring," he says, "because there aren't any herring or shad moving in the river. I like to use a very sharp Kahle hook and get as much bacon on it as I can. A sharp hook will cut through the bacon and give you a good hookset. And I've found that hickory-smoked bacon works best. Always."

The fish-finder rig is another Aziz favorite. This consists of a bass-casting sinker on the line above a barrel swivel. A short leader (up to 14-pound-test line), with a Kahle hook on the end and small Styrofoam ball in the middle, is tied to the swivel.

"The sinker holds the rig near bottom, and the ball floats your bait up a few inches where catfish can find it," Aziz says.

The only problem with these rigs, according to Aziz, is their propensity for attracting striped bass and smallmouths in summer.

"The best fishing for white cats is in spring and late fall when you're less likely to catch these other fish."

Small downriggers provide a means for catching white cats holding extremely deep in brackish water.

"We use light downriggers like those used on smaller lakes," he notes. "Your line is connected to the ball, which is dropped to the bottom in deep holes with current. Let out 6 to 7 feet of line away from the clamp so your bait bounces in the current a foot or so above the bottom. When a fish grabs the bait, it trips the clamp, releasing your line, and you set the hook. This is the best type of rig you can use in brackish water when you're anchored and fishing deep."

For Aziz and other cat fanatics in the Northeast, white cats are the essence of day-to-day fishing.

"We get a few channel catfish and some bullheads, too," he says. "But there are more white catfish up here than any other catfish. They're the best thing going in this part of the world. And anglers who learn how to catch them in the tidewater stretches of our big rivers will find fun and satisfaction day after day."

Blue Cats in Tidal Marshes

Barry Mullin of Nederland, Texas, fishes for winter blue cats in the brackish waters of coastal southeast Texas. His favorite honeyhole is Bessie Heights Marsh near the mouth of the Neches River. The Neches flows into Sabine Lake, a bay that empties into the Gulf of Mexico.

"This area of the river is the threshold between salt and freshwater," says Mullin. "There is a huge salt marsh on the east side of the river and some on the west.

"When there's plenty of rain," he continues, "the runoff purges all the saltwater out of the river and marsh. This sometimes happens in summer, and nearly always when the cold fronts make their way down in winter. In December, the blue cats begin showing up. The years when it rains a lot in fall, more catfish move down the river than normal."

Mullin fishes in deep holes in canals feeding the marsh. These holes occur wherever the tide enters the canals from the shallows.

"When the weather is mild, and the shallow-water temperature is warmer than the canals, blue cats often move into 2 feet of water or less in the open marsh," Mullin reports. "I look for places where the tide has cut trenches in the shallow marsh. A trench in shallow water is likely to hold blue cats, especially if it's near a hump covered with submerged grass. Blue cats are attracted to baitfish that hide in the grass and eat algae growing on the grass and mud.

"I use cut-bait to give the fish a scent trail to follow and usually catch baitfish that are abundant in the area I'm fishing—typically mullet, shad, or croakers. Shrimp also are good bait. I often chum with the same type bait I'm using. I start with a bait the length of my thumbnail on a No. 4 Kahle hook. If I'm catching too many little cats, I double the bait size. At times, the bigger blues want live bait only."

Blue cats position themselves to intercept baitfish being carried by the tide. Mullins says an incoming tide is best when fishing the shallow flats. When the tide is leaving the marsh, the catfish hold in holes created by swift current entering the canals. Catfish in Bessie Heights rarely bite when the tide is still.

"The most I've caught in one day has been twenty-three keeper-size blues, the biggest being 15 pounds. Four or five keeper-size fish is a normal day. I have caught several blues in the 12- to 15-pound range, and know of one 32-pound blue caught in one of the canals."

We have a lot yet to learn about catfish in tidal waters, but the tactics outlined here can help you catch brackish-water cats now. Check with your state fisheries department to determine which tidal rivers harbor catfish, then put your newfound knowledge to work this season.

C-C-Cats in the C-C-Cold: Joe Drose

In the world of catfishing, South Carolina's Santee Cooper lakes are hallowed water. This 170,000-acre dual reservoir system—lakes Marion and Moultrie—is a phenomenal fishery that not only produces big cats, but lots of them.

The current world-record channel cat of 58 pounds was caught here in 1958, but trophy-class channels haven't been plentiful since the 1960s. Nevertheless, 5- to 10-pounders make up a large part of the catch, and it's not unusual to catch a hundred or more daily.

Blue cats are found here as perhaps nowhere else. A 109-pounder, the former world record, was taken on rod and reel from the Cooper River just below the dam in 1991, and local guides claim some swimming the lakes today could be 30 to 40 pounds heavier. Fifty-, 60-, and 70-pound blues are caught so frequently that they hardly draw attention.

Giant flatheads also roam these world famous lakes. The 79-pound, 4-ounce state record was caught in the Santee Cooper Diversion Canal in 2001, and flatheads over 50 pounds are caught with surprising consistency.

The best fishing for these bruisers, however, is during the warm months. In the dead of winter, most anglers are targeting trophy blues and channels.

"Blues and channel cats aren't like us," says catfishing guide Joe Drose of Pineville, South Carolina. "They don't care how cold it is, so winter fishing for them in Marion and Moultrie can be outstanding. It's not unusual to catch several cats a day over 20 pounds, even when the temperature is freezing."

Drose should know. He's been guiding Santee Cooper catfish anglers for more than half a century.

On this day, he's sitting behind the wheel of his huge party barge, smiling, keeping a close watch on four rods in holders on the bow. A cold breeze is blowing across an open expanse of Lake Marion where we're fishing. Along with my catfishing companions, Lewis Peeler and Mark Davis, I'm enjoying the warmth of the boat's cabin. A transparent boat cover breaks the wind, turning away the February chill as we fish for giant cats.

So far, our luck hasn't been as good. We've landed two 5-pound-plus channel cats, but the monster cats refuse to bite. Frequently, we see a huge black blip on the screen of Drose's sonar—a big catfish lying on the bottom. Drose blames their lack of activity on a low-pressure system that's moving through the area.

"I read results of a study a Tennessee fisheries biologist did years ago," he tells me. "He said that when a low pressure system moves in, it affects a fish's swim bladder. Makes him feel just like you feel when you're nauseated. He'll just settle down on the bottom and won't feed till he's feeling better. It may be true, maybe not. But it makes as much sense as anything I've heard."

Suddenly, one of the rods on the boat's bow takes a nosedive. Lewis is beside it and makes the hookset. Something hefty surges away, stripping 30-pound line off the spool. "Feels like a good one," he says. "But not a monster."

The fish puts on an impressive show of bulldog battling, but Lewis soon swings it over the transom. It's another nice channel cat, 7, perhaps 8, pounds.

"Where's your grandpappy?" Lewis asks, twisting the hook from the fish's lip.

What surprises me most is how icy cold these fish are. Each fights like the dickens, yet when we touch one fresh out of the water, it feels like a frozen popsicle. How, I wonder, can a cold-blooded creature put up such a fight when its body temperature is barely above freezing? Antifreeze, perhaps?

Surprising, too, is Drose's fishing technique. In winter, he focuses his efforts in shallow water, fishing broad flats that border the edges of deeper creek channels. Most of the time we're fishing in 2 to 6 feet of water, far shallower than I expected to find winter fish. Drose explains:

"The vast majority of the catfish we catch in winter are blues and channels," he notes. "Flatheads just bury themselves in the bottom mud and sit there. They don't start biting well until May when the water warms up. Blues and channels, however, are active feeders year-round. I've caught them when it was so bone-cold out here that you could hardly reel one in once you'd hooked it."

Shallow-Water Fishing

Drose's winter catfishing techniques are easily duplicated by any angler who wants to waylay a trophy-class, cold-water catfish in a big, shallow reservoir. Because winter catfish gather in small areas to feed this time of year, he usually anchors his boat and still-fishes using sturdy tackle—7-foot Shakespeare Ugly Stick Tiger Rods and Shakespeare baitcasting reels spooled with 25- to 80-pound-test monofilament line. The heavier line is used when fishing areas with lots of stumps and other cover to lessen the chance of a big cat breaking off.

Drose's primary winter fishing rig consists of an egg sinker on the main line above a barrel swivel, with an 8- to 12-inch leader connecting the swivel to a sturdy 3/0 to 5/0 Kahle hook baited with cut-bait, either shad or herring. He casts this bottom-fishing rig to likely spots such as mussel beds and allows it to sit for up to fifteen minutes. If no bite is forthcoming, Drose moves to another spot and tries again. Several rigs may be presented at each location, with the poles held in heavy-duty rod holders affixed to railing on the bow of Drose's party barge.

"Most of the time we use small herring for bait," he continues. "I cut each herring in chunks, making smaller baits from it. I use all the pieces, but for some reason, the head piece always seems to draw more strikes. I run the hook through the belly part of the fish, because that's the thinnest part and leaves more hook exposed. If you cover your whole hook with bait, when the fish bites, you don't have any hook left to hook him with. I prefer laser-sharpened Kahle hooks because they're a lot sharper than regular hooks. They'll hook fish that you might have missed otherwise."

On the water, Drose becomes a hunter, searching for big cats feeding in the shallows. Winter catfishing is almost like bass fishing, he says. The angler casts to a good-looking spot in shallow water and hopes for a strike. But if one isn't forthcoming, he doesn't just sit in one spot waiting for something to happen. He keeps on the move, trying one area then another, hunting for his prey. Some stretches of bank won't yield a single fish, but others may produce a big catfish on every cast.

"Generally, the rougher the water is the better the fishing is in shallow water, if you can get your boat properly anchored," Drose notes. "We do all our fishing throughout the year during daylight hours. When there's a sharp breeze, it's stirring up the bottom in the shallows, moving food around. The catfish don't pay as much attention to the boat then as they do when it's calm.

"We also seem to do better on clear, sunny days," he adds. "The fish move around more then, and you get a lot more action. When it's cloudy,

Joe Drose (left) helps a friend land a trophy blue cat caught in the dead of winter.

they'll get somewhere and just sit; they don't move around a lot. You have to drop a bait right in front of one to get a bite."

Blues and Shad

There are times, of course, when channel and blue catfish leave the shallows to feed. Such is the case when extended periods of severe cold cause shad die-offs. When the water temperature first dips below 45 degrees, usually in December or January, cold-stressed shad attract enormous concentrations of hungry catfish.

"As the shad start dying and filtering out of these schools, catfish move in by the hundreds and get under those big schools of baitfish," Drose reports. "They gorge on the crippled shad as they drift down out of the schools. This pattern may last three to four weeks at a time.

"When the temperature is right and this is happening, a catfisherman should ride around in his boat and watch his sonar until he finds a big school of baitfish. He then takes a cast net and throws over the school to collect his bait. The smaller shad seem to work best, those about an inch or two long. Hook two or three at a time on a single hook, running the hook through the eyes and leaving the barb exposed. Then lower your rig all the way to the bottom, reel it up from the bottom about a foot, and get ready for the action that's likely to follow. When the catfish are really gorging on shad, you can't use more than one rod per man because they're biting so fast."

Drift-Fishing

When other tactics aren't producing, Drose may try drift-fishing for Santee's big winter cats.

"Drift-fishing allows you to cover more water so you can find cats that aren't where you expect them," he says. "Sometimes, if you want to catch

The author's wife, Theresa, shows off a nice winter blue caught while drift-fishing on South Carolina's Lake Moultrie.

blues, you've got to take your bait to them; you can't wait for them to come to your bait."

Some fishermen have no idea what type of structure or cover is beneath the water where they are drifting. Drose prefers to watch a sonar fishfinder as he drifts with the wind or moves with a trolling motor, guiding his boat over and along structure where blue cats are likely to be. Blues may be roaming around, he says, but they'll still do most of their wandering around bottom channels, humps, and other bottom features.

"Most of the time, we're moving back and forth over underwater hills or ridges, moving the bait from 20 to 40 feet of water and back," he says.

"You never know for sure where the cats will be. Some days you catch most fish in shallower water. Some days most are in deeper water. Some days you'll catch them shallow and deep."

Drose uses one rig—a float rig—when drifting.

"The main line is run through the eye of a 1¼- to 1¾-ounce pencil weight," he says, "and a barrel swivel is tied below it to keep the weight from sliding down. A 4-foot leader is then tied to the lower eye of the swivel. A 2½-inch crappie float is added in the middle of the leader, and a 3/0 or 4/0 wide-bend Eagle Claw hook is tied at the end.

"The float suspends the baited hook above the bottom to help prevent snags," he continues. "By sliding the float up or down the leader, you can adjust the depth at which the bait floats, depending on what the catfish are doing. The bait we use is 4- to 5-inch whole blueback herring."

Drose has caught blue cats up to 70 pounds when drifting, and says it's common to catch trophy-class fish—30 pounds and up—using this method. He drifts with 100 yards of 25-pound-test line out to keep his rig moving smoothly across the bottom. With lesser lengths of line running behind the boat, the weight has a tendency to drag or snag, causing the bait to jump and move wildly about. Four 7- to 8-foot Shakespeare Tiger Rods held in rail-mounted rod holders are used for each drift. Each is outfitted with a Shakespeare Tidewater reel that holds up to 300 yards of 25-pound-test line.

"A high-capacity reel is a must," Drose notes. "If you have 100 yards of line out and a big blue hits, you better have plenty of line still on the reel or you could get spooled."

As mentioned, Drose fishes from a large party barge. To slow his drift, he employs one or two custom-made sea anchors (drift socks), each 6 feet in diameter, which are attached to the boat with short lengths of nylon rope. The wind pushes the craft along, while the sea anchors govern the drift speed.

"The best time for drift-fishing is when the water's white-capping some," he says. "You've got to have the sea anchors to control your speed or you'll go too fast. The anchors also help hold your boat straight so you have a controlled drift and not just a bouncy boat ride."

Before our day of fishing was over, I photographed Lewis and Mark grinning with 51- and 39-pound winter blue cats they pulled over the transom of Drose's party barge. Each put up an unforgettable battle. Each was popsicle-cold to the touch, just like the many jumbo channel cats we also caught that day.

"I love winter catfishing," says Drose. "You drop a bait down and reel it up a little, and often, before you set the rod in the holder, you'll have a big one on. Then the action really heats up, and all of a sudden you remember why you're out there fishing on such a cold day. There's nothing more fun and exciting."

Drose is right about that. When winter cats start biting, that frigid feeling disappears. Nothing's better for what ails you on a frosty day.

CHAPTER ELEVEN

The Three Dozen Best Catfishing Tips

Even the best catfish anglers have days when they feel catfish are finning their noses at them. Don't take it; fight back! Anyone can catch catfish when they're bunched up on a feeding foray. But when they're scattered, finicky, full-bellied, or disinterested, remember these suggestions—three dozen ways to improve success and turn a dismal day into a great one.

1. **Look at your hook.**

   Having trouble hooking catfish? First, be sure your hooks are needle-sharp. Run each point over a fingernail. Sharp hooks dig in. Those that skate across the nail without catching should be honed or replaced. Second, instead of burying your hook in bait, leave the barb exposed. Catfish won't notice, and more hookups will result.

2. **Rig right.**

   Learn a variety of rigs, and use each when appropriate. A simple egg-sinker rig may work great in a pond but not a river. Drift rigs may be

The author gives well-known angler Bill Dance some tips on how to hook and land a nice catfish.

needed when cats are scattered and hard to find. A specialty rig, like the float-paternoster, is best when fishing large live baits. Learn more rigs, catch more cats.

3. Use accessories for night fishing.

When night fishing, know when a cat takes your bait. Helpful products include: night bobbers (special floats with a light on top powered by a cyalume light stick or lithium battery); a 12-volt ultraviolet light, which makes fluorescent monofilament glow, allowing you to see line movements; rods with glow-in-the-dark or fluorescent tips; rod bells, which clip on and ring when a catfish shakes your pole; and electronic bite indicators, which attach to your line and emit an audible signal when a catfish runs with your bait.

4. Get underwater eyes.

A sonar fish-finder helps pinpoint catfish you'd otherwise miss and is a must-have piece of equipment for locating underwater structure and catfish. Buy one, learn to use it, and use it often.

Many anglers stay off the water during winter, mistakenly believing catfish can't be caught in this season.

5. **Get a net.**

You can land small cats with your line or hands. But for trophy cats, always carry an oversized landing net with a large reinforced hoop, long handle (at least 48 inches) and a long net (48 inches or more).

6. **Get chummy with them.**

Where legal, use chum to attract more cats to your fishing holes. Place a gallon of wheat in a plastic container and cover with water. Place in a sunny location outdoors, uncovered. Allow it to sit several days until the mixture sours. Scatter handfuls of the fermented mix in several areas prior to fishing. Lower your regular bait to the bottom with the grain, and prepare for action.

7. **Know when to go fishing.**

Catfish can be caught night and day, but there are some general rules for maximizing success. Fishing clear waters on cloudy days works, but if skies are clear, wait and fish after dark. In low-clarity waters, fish when you like, day or night. Catfish activity often peaks at dawn, so it may pay to try then. Flatheads are more nocturnal than channels or blues; for them, night fishing usually works best.

8. Fish often, year-round.

Some anglers mistakenly believe catfishing is best during summer, but other seasons may be more productive. Those who regularly catch trophy blue cats often do so by fishing deep ledges in winter. And normally sedentary flatheads roam and feed ravenously during high water in spring, and again in autumn, prior to entering a period of winter torpor. Channel cats bite spring, summer, fall, and winter. Ice fishermen often catch them. The worst time to fish? In summer when cats are spawning. Egg-laying females and nest-guarding males are in cavities and may not feed at all.

9. Keep moving.

Catfishing often becomes a "sit-and-wait" game, with an immobile angler and stationary bait. But in many situations, you'll catch more fish if you and your bait keep moving. Try drift-fishing tactics if you have a boat, or drifting a bait beneath a bobber when bankfishing. You'll cover more water and find more fish.

10. Fight up, not out.

To land more big cats, fight them up not out. For instance, imagine you're fishing a ledge where shallow water drops into deep water. In this situation, it's best to position your boat over the deeper water. That way, if you hook a fish on the ledge, you can pull it into the hole and fight up not out. If you do the opposite, pulling the cat from deep water to shallow, it will be much more difficult to land.

11. Don't cast a shadow.

Catfish spook when a shadow crosses the water. Keep the sun in your face or to your side, not at your back, to avoid casting a shadow on the water you're fishing. And don't fish directly under your boat in clear waters.

Big catfish require big nets, and lots of help, to land.

12. Near or far?

On moonless nights, catfish hunt the shallows. Cast your bait near shore, not toward deeper water. On moonlit nights, start deep and work into progressively shallower water until you find fish. Tighten your line, keep a finger on it to detect bites, and set the hook hard when you get a taker.

13. Fish the morning shift.

Catfishermen often disregard one of the best fishing times—dawn. On many waters, catfish activity peaks just as the sun rises. Be fishing at daybreak, and your catch rate may soar.

14. Lighten up.

When you want to catch lots of cats, even if they're small, fish light tackle—a 6- to 7-foot, light or ultralight rod; an ultralight spinning or spincast reel; 4- to 8-pound-test line; split shot; size 1/0 to 3/0 hooks. Light tackle is less likely to spook wary fish, and all cats you catch will fight like whoppers.

15. Be there when they chow down.

Among the best ponds to fish are those where catfish are fed a supplemental diet of commercial catfish chow. Pond owners often set the timers on their automatic feeders to dispense food at regular hours throughout the day. Catfish quickly learn when feeding time is, and any bait dropped in the water just prior to feeding hour will be promptly gobbled up by waiting cats. Be sure, of course, to request permission before fishing private waters.

16. Understand weather effects.

During periods of stormy weather, some catfishermen get frustrated trying to figure out the best fishing patterns. One day, catfish may seem ravenous; the next, they have lockjaw. As a general rule, the best fishing is right before a storm when

Opposite: This trophy blue cat, caught by the author's son, Josh, was taken just before a storm front passed through, a prime time to fish for these whiskered warriors.

Catching giant catfish like this doesn't happen every day. Anglers must be persistent to enjoy success.

atmospheric pressure begins to drop, although this pattern won't always hold true. Catfish often quit feeding the day or two before a front appears and seem insatiable when it arrives. Feeding activity peaks as the front approaches and remains at a high level until it passes through. On the day after the storm has passed, fishing success is usually off considerably, but a day or two later, the cats will be back to normal feeding patterns. Be ready to hit the water when there's a falling barometer reading combined with a south to east wind, indicators of a weather change ahead.

17. **Set your drag.**

One of the biggest mistakes you can make when targeting trophy cats is forgetting to properly set your drag. A big whiskerfish will snap even 80-pound line if the drag is cranked down too tight, and a monster can throw a bird's nest in your line or spool you if the drag is set too low. Remember to set your drag at a point just below the breaking strength of your line every time out.

For bankfishing, it's important to set up near cover and structure likely to attract catfish.

18. Watch the birds.

If catfishing is slow, watch for flocks of seabirds plummeting from the sky into the water. Gulls, terns, and other birds often feed on schools of shad and other baitfish being driven to the surface by white bass, largemouths, stripers, etc. Catfish often hang out under this type of action, feeding on crippled bait drifting to the bottom. Move in and catch them.

19. Be persistent.

Persistence is one of the most important qualities of anglers who frequently catch trophy catfish. Anyone can learn the tactics necessary for catching cats, but to catch a trophy-class fish, you have to keep bait in the water where the big ones swim. Learn everything you can about a lake or river, and then fish it day after day after day, learning more. Catfishermen who do that have the best chance of catching the catfish of a lifetime.

20. Hold tight.

If you place your rod in a rod holder, be sure it's firmly anchored. Likewise, keep a firm grip on handheld tackle. A big cat can yank a rod and reel into the water quicker than you can say "Boo."

21. Care for your line.

Be sure to change your fishing line regularly, and check it every time you catch a fish to see if it's scarred up and needs to be replaced. Many anglers hook huge catfish but aren't prepared to land them. Don't be among them.

22. Wade on in.

Many small, seldom-fished streams harbor lots of nice catfish. Wade-fishing is often the best way to catch a mess in these environs. Slip into waders or a pair of shorts and tennis shoes and move slowly through the stream, stopping to cast bait to fallen trees, ledges, and eddy pools where cats may hide.

23. Be flexible in your presentations.

Don't stick to a single presentation if it's not producing cats. If one bait doesn't work, try another. Change to a bigger or smaller bait. Vary the depth at which it is presented. If catfish are biting, and you've come prepared with an assortment of baits and tactics, sooner or later you'll pinpoint something productive.

24. Use proper boat placement when still-fishing.

When still-fishing from a boat, carry two anchors to position your craft sideways in good holes. This way your rods are spread out to cover more water and avoid tangles. Try to pinpoint prime catfishing areas such as channel edges and humps, and then narrow your fishing zones to a few best spots—a stump field near the channel edge, for example, or a large snag along a riprapped bank. Position your boat for best access to the structure you've chosen, then cast your bait to that spot and wait for a bite.

25. Pick the right spot.

When catfishing from shore, it's important to set up where action will be best. The area just below a river dam provides some of the best cat action, especially if you can cast to the slack-water areas between open gates. Many bank fishermen set up below tributaries or at the junction of two rivers. Fishing near fallen trees at the head of a deep pool on an outside bend of the river also can lead to good catches.

26. Float right.

Use a long rod and keep your rod tip high when drifting a float rig. This keeps most of the line off the water, resulting in better rig control and hooksets.

27. Keep notes.

Regardless of where or how you fish, when you establish a productive pattern, tuck it away in your memory for future reference. Better yet, write it in a fishing journal or key it into a computer diary. If you visit the same body of water, or one similar to it, during the same time period under similar weather conditions, chances are good the same fishing pattern will bring you luck again.

28. Clear water? Use light line.

Catfish usually aren't line shy, but in clear water lighter lines offer several advantages. First, you gain extra yardage on your casts. This helps you maintain more distance from your fishing area so catfish aren't spooked by shadows or movements. Smaller-diameter lines also have less resistance in water, so your bait sinks quicker, hurrying to the depths where catfish are likely to be. Finally, light lines aren't as likely to be noticed by unusually spooky catfish, thus increasing your chances of a successful hookup.

29. Try piers.

Fishing piers offer fishing opportunities for everyone. Nearly all are wheelchair-accessible, so the joys of catfishing from these man-made hotspots can be experienced despite mobility limitations. Piers also provide safe, convenient locations where you can take the whole family catfishing. Pack a picnic lunch, outfit your children with life jackets to avoid any unforeseen mishaps, then share the fun and excitement of catfishing, pier-style.

30. When preparing stinkbaits, beware.

The use of plastic containers is recommended when mixing and storing stinkbaits. This is because some stinkbait concoctions give off fermentation bubbles and gases that can cause a tightly sealed glass or metal container to explode, with dangerous and gut-wrenching results. Also, never tighten a lid on the mixture, and store all stinkbait mixtures outside at all times.

31. Take plenty of hooks for bullheads.

Bullheads are notorious hook swallowers, so carry plenty of hooks when fishing for them. You can remove hooks with a disgorger or long-nosed pliers, but it's quicker to cut the line and retrieve hooks when cleaning your catch. Better yet, use small circle hooks, which tend to hook the fish in the corner of the mouth and are easy to remove.

32. Treat pokes right.

If you get poked by a catfish's sharp pectoral or dorsal fin spines, old-timers recommend swiping the fish's belly across the wound to neutralize the stinging sensation. Household ammonia daubed on the wound has the same effect.

33. Be patient.

Catching trophy catfish doesn't happen every day, even for those thoroughly familiar with their everyday habits. You may spend many fishless hours trying to hook a trophy fish. Learn to bide your time without getting unduly upset. Get comfortable and relax. It could be hours before a big one bites, but sooner or later, the patient catter reaps his reward.

34. Bait up with clean hands.

Be very careful not to handle catfish baits if you get things like sunscreen, insect repellent, or gasoline on your hands. Even a little dab will make cats look elsewhere for dinner.

35. Enjoy yourself.

Bring some chairs, drinks, and friends on your bankfishing forays. Build a campfire, kick back, and chew the fat. The camaraderie and relaxation are what make this form of catfishing so much fun. Catching cats is just a bonus.

36. Conserve cats.

"Today's releases are tomorrow's trophies." That's the motto of all anglers who regularly catch cats that others envy. Keep smaller cats to eat if you're fish hungry; release those over 5 pounds.

Opposite: Sitting by a campfire with friends while waiting for a fish to bite is one of the most enjoyable forms of catfishing.

CHAPTER TWELVE

Preparing Catfish

With a little know-how, cleaning catfish for the table is a task that can be accomplished with relative ease. Be sure, however, to avoid the sharp pectoral and dorsal fins throughout the cleaning process.

How to Fillet a Catfish

Filleting is the simplest cleaning process and produces boneless pieces of meat. This can be done with nothing more than a good, sharp knife. An electric fillet knife will make it even easier.

Begin by laying the fish on its side on a cutting board or other flat, hard surface. To get the fish to lie flat on its side, it you may have to place the fish so that the stiff side (pectoral) fin sticks through a hole or crack in the surface beneath it.

Begin filleting by placing the knife at the rear edge of the pectoral fin. Slice downward to the backbone, then turn the knife blade toward the tail and continue cutting, staying on top of the dorsal and anal fins. Continue your cut toward the tail until you have almost, but not quite, removed the fillet.

With the fillet barely attached to the tail, flip it away from the fish. Position your knife on the narrow portion of the fillet, and while pulling the fish away from the knife, slice between the meat and the skin to remove the fillet. Now flip the fish over and fillet the other side. The fillets can be used whole or cut crosswise into smaller "fingers."

How to Skin a Catfish

Many catfish anglers prefer skinning the fish and preparing them pan-dressed (to be cooked whole) or cut into steaks. This requires a sharp knife and skinning pliers. Regular pliers can be used, but skinning pliers have wider jaws that afford a better grip on the catfish's thin, slippery skin.

Catfish are easier to skin if they're hung tail down from an overhead support or from a nail protruding outward from a board attached to the wall or a post. Hanging the fish also allows you to cut off the tail and let the fish bleed out into a bucket placed beneath it. This makes the flesh whiter and firmer.

Begin skinning by making a circular cut through the skin behind the head. Starting just behind the pectoral fin on one side of the fish, run the cut up, over, and down to the other pectoral fin. Next, with the point of the knife, split the skin down the middle of the back, from head to tail, going down one side or the other of the dorsal fin. Now split the skin on the other side of the dorsal fin, connecting this cut to the one just made. The fish is now ready for skinning.

Grasp the skin with the pliers and pull it toward the tail. It should strip off in one or two pieces. Repeat the process on the other side. If you wish to save the fatty but delicious piece of belly flesh, you also can remove the belly skin and then cut away the boneless belly meat.

Remove the head using a heavy knife or cleaver to sever the backbone. Remove the pectoral fins with the head. The fish now should be gutted and the fins removed. The adipose fin and tail are simply sliced off. To remove the dorsal and anal fins, grip each at its rear edge with the skinning pliers and lift toward the head of the fish, pulling the fin from the body.

Finally, remove all dark-red flesh along the lateral line. Contaminants that may be in the water where the catfish was caught tend to concentrate in this meat, which often has a strong flavor. Small cats (12 inches or less) are now ready to rinse and cook. Larger fish should be cut crosswise into ½- to 1-inch-thick steaks.

After the fish are cleaned, they can be cooked and eaten, or you can store the fillets, steaks, or pan-dressed fish in the freezer until you're ready to prepare them. To avoid freezer burn and preserve freshness, immerse the prepared fish in water when you freeze them (either in zip-seal plastic freezer bags or plastic containers); better yet, vacuum-seal them using a product such as the Tilia FoodSaver.

Cooking Catfish

Catfish has a mild, sweet taste and flaky texture that make it a favorite on the dinner table. In the Deep South, catfish is almost always cooked by dredging in seasoned cornmeal and then deep-frying. Folks say there's simply no tastier method of preparation, so why bother with anything else? The truth is, catfish is wonderfully adaptable and complements most cooking techniques. Fried catfish is delicious, but catfish also can be grilled, baked, sautéed, blackened, poached, or combined with other foods for casseroles and chowders. You're limited only by your imagination.

The biggest mistake made by many catfish cooks is overcooking. Catfish is naturally tender and cooks quickly. It's done when it flakes easily with a fork.

The following recipes offer a variety of ways to add the delectable flavor of catfish to your menus.

FRIED CATFISH, ARKANSAS STYLE

2 pounds catfish fillets, steaks, or whole fish
1 small bottle Louisiana hot sauce, or to taste
4 cups milk
¾ cup yellow cornmeal
¼ cup flour
2 teaspoons salt
½ teaspoon cayenne pepper
½ teaspoon garlic powder
Peanut oil

1. Marinate fish 1 hour in a large bowl in which the hot sauce and milk have been mixed. Remove fish and drain.
2. Combine the dry ingredients by shaking them together in a large plastic bag. Add the fish, and shake to coat.
3. Put a couple of inches of peanut oil in a deep-fryer and heat to 365°F. Add pieces of fish in a single layer, and fry until fish flakes easily with a fork, about 5 to 6 minutes.
4. Remove and drain on paper towels. Repeat with remaining fish.

Serves 4.

BAKED CATFISH ALMANDINE

½ cup whole almonds, toasted
3 tablespoons cornmeal
2 tablespoons grated Parmesan cheese
2 tablespoons chopped fresh parsley
1 tablespoon flour
Salt and freshly ground black pepper, to taste
2 tablespoons fresh lemon juice
2 pounds catfish fillets
Parsley sprigs and lemon wedges for garnish

1. Grind the almonds and combine with the cornmeal, Parmesan cheese, flour, salt, and pepper.
2. Sprinkle the lemon juice over the catfish, and coat the fillets thoroughly with the almond mixture.
3. Place the fillets on a baking sheet and bake at 400°F for 8 minutes or until fish flakes easily with a fork.

Serves 4.

CAT CAKES WITH DIJON SAUCE

1 tablespoon chopped green pepper

4 tablespoons chopped green onion

½ cup vegetable oil

1 pound cooked, flaked catfish fillets

1 egg, beaten

1 tablespoon mayonnaise

6 tablespoons dry breadcrumbs

1 teaspoon dry mustard

¼ teaspoon ground black pepper

¼ teaspoon cayenne pepper

1 teaspoon seasoned salt

1. Sauté green pepper and green onion in 2 tablespoons oil until soft. Drain.
2. Mix peppers and onions with remaining ingredients. Chill for at least 20 minutes.
3. Form into patties and cook in the remaining oil until golden brown on each side. Serve with Dijon sauce.

Serves 4–6.

Dijon Sauce

½ cup plain yogurt

3 tablespoons dry mustard

¼ cup mayonnaise

1 tablespoon chopped green onion

2 tablespoons dill pickle relish

2 tablespoons balsamic vinegar

Mix all ingredients and chill until ready to serve. Serve at room temperature.

BLACKENED CATFISH

Blackening Spice

2 tablespoons paprika

2 tablespoons salt

2 teaspoons onion powder

2 teaspoons garlic powder

2 teaspoons cayenne pepper

1½ teaspoons white pepper

1½ teaspoons black pepper

1 teaspoon dried thyme leaves

1 teaspoon dried oregano leaves

10 (6- to 10-ounce) catfish fillets (not more than ¾-inch thick)

1 pound unsalted butter, melted and kept warm in a skillet

1. Use a fork to thoroughly combine blackening spice ingredients in a small bowl.
2. Heat a large cast-iron skillet until it is almost white hot.
3. Dip each piece of fish in melted butter, then sprinkle some blackening spice mix evenly on each side. Immediately place the fish in the hot skillet, cooking one piece at a time. Pour a teaspoon of melted butter atop the fish. (Be careful; the butter may flame up.)
4. Cook about 2 minutes, turn, and pour another teaspoon of butter on top. Cook 2 minutes more.
5. When the fish is done, it should be flaky, white, and still very moist inside.
6. Serve each piece while piping hot with more hot melted butter on the side for dipping.

Serves 10.

CATFISH POORBOYS

6 large crusty rolls

1 cup ketchup

3 dashes Tabasco sauce

1 tablespoon prepared mustard

1 tablespoon minced onion

6 fried catfish fillets

Dill pickles

1. Cut rolls in half lengthwise and scoop out the soft centers; place rolls in the oven until hot but not crispy.
2. Combine ketchup, Tabasco, mustard, and onion.
3. Spread each hot roll with this mixture, then top with catfish, dill pickles, and the top of the roll.

Serves 6.

MICROWAVE CATFISH EN PAPILLOTE

3 tablespoons dry sherry

1 tablespoon soy sauce

2 tablespoons chopped green onion

1 clove garlic, minced

¼ teaspoon ground ginger

Parchment paper

Olive oil or butter

4 (6-ounce) catfish fillets

1 red pepper, cut in thin strips

2 ounces ham, cut in thin strips

8 lemon slices

1. Combine the first five ingredients in a bowl.

2. Cut four 12- by 15-inch sheets of parchment paper. Fold each sheet crosswise in half to crease, then unfold. Trim the edges to create a heart shape if desired, and brush one side with a little olive oil or butter. Place one fillet on the oiled side of each sheet.

3. Top each fillet with one-fourth of the red pepper strips and ham strips and with two lemon slices. Spoon one-fourth of the sauce over each, then crimp and seal the edges of each packet.

4. Arrange two packets on a microwave-safe plate. Microwave on high 6 minutes. Let stand 1 minute. Repeat with remaining two packets.

5. Arrange packets on serving plates; open carefully at table. Serve immediately.

(For conventional oven cooking, preheat oven to 425°F. Place crimped packets on a baking sheet; bake for 10–12 minutes.)

30-MINUTE CAJUN CATFISH

1 tablespoon vegetable oil
1 small green pepper, diced
½ teaspoon dried oregano leaves, crushed
1 can (10¾ ounce) Campbell's Condensed
  Tomato Soup
⅓ cup water
⅛ teaspoon garlic powder
⅛ teaspoon ground black pepper
⅛ teaspoon ground red pepper
1 pound catfish fillets
Hot cooked rice

1. Heat oil in a skillet.
2. Add green pepper and oregano; cook until tender-crisp.
3. Add soup, water, garlic powder, black pepper, and red pepper. Heat to a boil.
4. Add catfish fillets; cover, and cook over low heat 5 minutes or until done. Serve with rice.

Serves 4.

CATFISH STIR-FRY

2 tablespoons sesame or peanut oil
2 carrots, thinly sliced
1 onion, thinly sliced
2 zucchini squash, thinly sliced
1 teaspoon chopped parsley
½ teaspoon thyme
1 pound catfish fillets, cut in 1-inch pieces
¼ teaspoon black pepper
Hot cooked rice

1. In a wok or large skillet, heat oil. Add vegetables, parsley, and thyme; stir-fry until slightly tender.
2. Season catfish with pepper and add to the pan.
3. Stir-fry until fish is opaque and flakes easily. Serve over a bed of hot rice.

Serves 4.

EASY GRILLED CATFISH

Any number of catfish fillets
Melted butter
Lemon pepper

1. Dip the fish fillets in melted butter, and season to taste with lemon pepper.
2. Place catfish in a well-oiled grill basket or on a well-oiled grill rack.
3. Grill on an uncovered grill directly over medium-hot coals about 5 minutes per side or until fish flakes easily.

CHAPTER THIRTEEN

Conservation

In some states, catfish still are considered rough fish, and you can legally keep as many as you want—10, 20, 100, 500. Length limits are unheard of in many parts of the U.S.

Commercial fishing is also unregulated in many areas. On two of the country's most famous trophy catfish lakes, for instance, commercial anglers are allowed to use trotlines to catch cats. As long as they buy the proper tags, each can use up to two thousand hooks. It's not unusual in these lakes to see a commercial fisherman unloading a boat containing one hundred or more catfish over 30 pounds.

Unfortunately, facts such as these lead many anglers to believe that harvest restrictions are unnecessary; i.e., if the state says it's OK, then there must be plenty of catfish to support such practices. And after all, excellent populations of catfish remain all around the country, even in many heavily fished waters. So why should we bother with restrictions?

At one time, our country's bass anglers were asking the same question. Most of them used hit-and-miss fishing tactics, just as most of today's catfish anglers do. And bass seemed a limitless resource. How could we possibly hurt their numbers?

Savvy catfish fans keep only smaller fish to eat and release the trophies they catch to fight another day.

Enter the modern age of bass fishing. Around the early 1970s, a wide variety of sophisticated fishing equipment suddenly became available to the average bass angler: depthfinders, more effective lures, better rods and reels, and other more effective gear. Anglers also were flooded with more and more information on how to catch more bass—in magazines and books, on television, on videos. All this enabled bass anglers to become more skillful and efficient.

As bassing became more popular, we learned that sport fishermen *could* adversely impact the quality of fishing by removing too many fish. Catch-and-release fishing, once scorned, quickly became the norm. Under pressure from sport fishermen, states started implementing more restrictive harvest regulations to protect and enhance our bass fisheries. Now it's unusual to find a body of water that *doesn't* have a variety of harvest restrictions for bass—slot limits, length limits, catch-and-release only, etc.

Catfishing is now at a similar crossroads. The day is coming soon when many more catfish anglers will have the ability to consistently make outstanding catches. With the rising popularity of the sport, and as catfishermen become more skillful and efficient, the need for voluntary and mandatory harvest restrictions will become greater. The question is, will fisheries managers and catfishermen apply the lessons learned with other fish before catfish populations are harmed?

To a large extent, the answer to that question depends on you. Changes won't be realized until catfishermen actively work to bring them about. You can help by contacting your elected and appointed representatives and communicating your concerns. Let them know that catfish are more than rough fish. They're among the most popular sportfish in the nation, and properly managed sport fisheries can generate millions of dollars for a state's economy.

Voluntary catch-and-release fishing is a good way to protect and perpetuate our outstanding trophy catfishing opportunities. Keep smaller fish to eat if you like, but release older, less common trophies to be caught again.

Be sure to do it right. Catfish are extremely hardy. An individual may live for hours out of the water. But if you expect a cat to survive following release, it's important to handle it properly. Follow these simple tips, and you can greatly increase the chances the fish you turn back will remain healthy and available for you or some other fisherman to land again.

- Use barbless hooks, or crimp the barbs with pliers.
- Bring the fish to the boat quickly; don't play the fish to total exhaustion while attempting to land it.
- Hold the fish in the water as much as possible when handling it, removing the hook and preparing it for release.
- Wet your hands so you don't remove the protective slime coating the fish.
- If the fish has swallowed the hook, don't pull it out. Rather, cut the line as close to the hook as possible, leaving the hook inside the fish.
- Don't squeeze the fish or put your fingers in its gills. Cradle it in the water and move it back and forth to oxygenate the gills. When the fish is properly rested, it will swim from your hands.

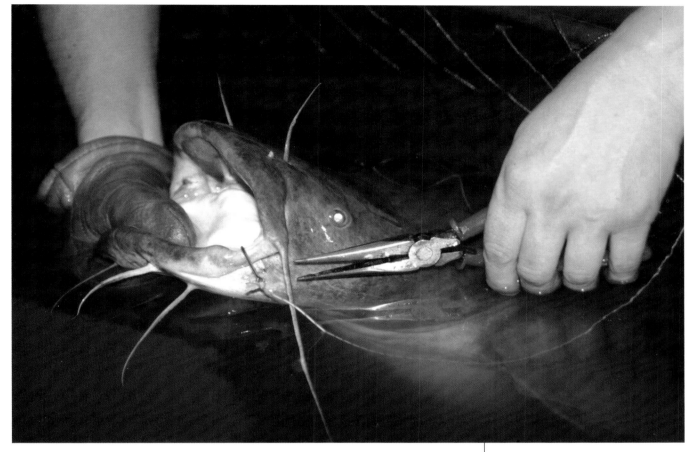

Keep catfish you plan to release in the water as much as possible and handle with care.

The best catfishing I ever enjoyed was on Manitoba's Red River, one of those rare catfish rivers where barbless hooks are required by law. The daily channel cat limit was four, none of which could exceed 24 inches. On a three-day fishing trip there, I caught around fifty channel cats, all of which were larger than any channel cat I had previously caught during a lifetime spent pursuing them. The smallest weighed approximately 17 pounds, the largest around 35 pounds.

I have often wondered: If a river in Canada, where the growing season is short, can produce such tremendous numbers of trophy catfish, what might a similar river in the U.S. produce if similar fishing restrictions were placed upon it? If more catfish anglers practice voluntary catch and release, if more of us push lawmakers to enact reasonable harvest restrictions, perhaps someday we'll have the answer to that question.

INDEX

ABOUT THE AUTHOR

Keith "Catfish" Sutton has been called the "Guru of Catfishing" and "Mr. Catfish," and with good reason. This is his third book about fishing for these

whiskered warriors. His forty-year pursuit of giant catfish has taken him from Canada to Mexico, Brazil, and Venezuela. He has fished for cats in half the states in the United States, in all seasons, day and night, with every bait and rig imaginable. His special insights about these incredible sportfish come from decades of on-the-water research and countless hours of discussions with master anglers, biologists, and researchers.

Sutton is a prolific freelance writer, photographer, editor and lecturer. His works have appeared in hundreds of books, magazines, newspapers, Web sites and scientific journals, including *Outdoor Life, Field & Stream, Sports Afield, In-Fisherman, North American Fisherman, Cabela's Outfitter Journal*, and others. He lives in Alexander, Arkansas, with his wife, Theresa. They have six sons.